The Public Understanding of Assessment

CW00818784

Assessment of educational achievement, whether by traditional examinations or by teachers in schools, attracts considerable public interest, particularly when it is associated with 'high stakes' outcomes such as university entry or selection for employment. When the individual's results do not chime with their or their teachers' expectations, doubts creep in about the process of assessment that has arrived at this result.

However, educational assessment is made up of many layers of complexity, which are not always clear to the general public, including teachers, students, and parents, and which are not easily understood outside of the expert assessment community. These layers may be organized in highly co-dependent relationships that include reliability, validity, human judgment, and errors, and the uses and interpretations of the various types of assessment. No-one could reasonably argue that the principles and complexities of educational assessment should be core learning in public education, but there is a growing realization that trust in the UK assessment system is under some threat as the media and others sensationalize or politicize any problems that arise each year.

This book offers the first comprehensive overview of how the general public is considered to perceive and understand a wide variety of aspects of educational assessment, and how this understanding may be improved. This book was originally published as a special issue of the *Oxford Review of Education*.

John Gardner is a Professor of Education and Senior Deputy Principal of the University of Stirling, UK. His research interests include policy and practice in all sectors of education, particularly in relation to assessment. He has over 120 academic publications and has authored or co-authored seven books, including the most recent editorship of the four-volume *Assessment in Education* (2014). From 1994–2010, he was a member of the globally influential Assessment Reform Group, and he is currently a visiting professor at the Oxford University Centre for Educational Assessment. He is a fellow of the Chartered Institute of Educational Assessors and a fellow of the Academy of Social Sciences. In 2011, he completed a two-year term as President of the British Educational Research Association, and from 2011–2014 he was a member of the Education panel of the Research Excellence Framework, REF 2014.

The Public Understanding of Assessment

Edited by
John Gardner

LONDON AND NEW YORK

First published 2016
by Routledge

2 Park Square, Milton Park, Abingdon, Oxfordshire OX14 4RN
711 Third Avenue, New York, NY 10017

Routledge is an imprint of the Taylor & Francis Group, an informa business

First issued in paperback 2017

Chapters 2–5 and 7–9 © 2016 Taylor & Francis

Chapter 1 © 2013 Onora O'Neill

Chapter 6 © 2013 Cambridge Assessment

British Library Cataloguing in Publication Data
A catalogue record for this book is available from the British Library

ISBN 13: 978-1-138-18877-8 (hbk)
ISBN 13: 978-1-138-30896-1 (pbk)

Typeset in Plantin
by diacriTech, Chennai

Publisher's Note
The publisher accepts responsibility for any inconsistencies that may have
arisen during the conversion of this book from journal articles to book
chapters, namely the possible inclusion of journal terminology.

Disclaimer
Every effort has been made to contact copyright holders for their
permission to reprint material in this book. The publishers would be
grateful to hear from any copyright holder who is not here acknowledged
and will undertake to rectify any errors or omissions in future editions of
this book.

Contents

CONTENTS

Citation Information

The chapters in this book were originally published in the *Oxford Review of Education*, volume 39, issue 1 (February 2013). When citing this material, please use the original page numbering for each article, as follows:

Introduction
John Gardner
Oxford Review of Education, volume 39, issue 1 (February 2013) pp. 1–3

Chapter 1
Intelligent accountability in education
Onora O'Neill
Oxford Review of Education, volume 39, issue 1 (February 2013) pp. 4–16

Chapter 2
Perceptions of trust in public examinations
Lucy Simpson and Jo-Anne Baird
Oxford Review of Education, volume 39, issue 1 (February 2013) pp. 17–35

Chapter 3
Towards improving public understanding of judgement practice in standards-referenced assessment: an Australian perspective
Val Klenowski
Oxford Review of Education, volume 39, issue 1 (February 2013) pp. 36–51

Chapter 4
The public understanding of assessment in educational reform in the United States
Susan M. Brookhart
Oxford Review of Education, volume 39, issue 1 (February 2013) pp. 52–71

Chapter 5
The public understanding of error in educational assessment
John Gardner
Oxford Review of Education, volume 39, issue 1 (February 2013) pp. 72–92

Chapter 6

Ofqual's Reliability Programme: a case study exploring the potential to improve public understanding and confidence
Paul E. Newton
Oxford Review of Education, volume 39, issue 1 (February 2013) pp. 93–113

Chapter 7

Communication strategies for enhancing qualification users' understanding of educational assessment: recommendations from other public interest fields
Suzanne Chamberlain
Oxford Review of Education, volume 39, issue 1 (February 2013) pp. 114–127

Chapter 8

Misleading the public understanding of assessment: wilful or wrongful interpretation by government and media
Warwick Mansell
Oxford Review of Education, volume 39, issue 1 (February 2013) pp. 128–138

Chapter 9

Media roles in influencing the public understanding of educational assessment issues
Roger Murphy
Oxford Review of Education, volume 39, issue 1 (February 2013) pp. 139–150

For any permission-related enquiries please visit:
http://www.tandfonline.com/page/help/permissions

Notes on Contributors

Jo-Anne Baird is Professor of Educational Assessment at Oxford University, UK, and Director of the Oxford University Centre for Educational Assessment. Her research interests are on examination standards, assessment policy, rater effects, and systemic assessment issues.

Susan M. Brookhart is an independent educational consultant based in Helena, Montana, USA, and Senior Research Associate at the Center for Advancing the Study of Teaching and Learning in the School of Education at Duquesne University, Pittsburgh, Pennsylvania, USA. She was 2007–2009 editor of *Educational Measurement: Issues and Practice,* a journal of the National Council on Measurement in Education. Her interests include the role of both formative and summative classroom assessment in student motivation and achievement, the connection between classroom assessment and large-scale assessment, and grading.

Suzanne Chamberlain is Education and Assessment Lead at the National School of Healthcare Science, Birmingham, UK. In this role she works closely with key colleagues across multiple healthcare science specialisms to develop quality assessments for clinical scientists at various levels as part of the Modernising Scientific Careers initiative for Health Education England. This includes the design and implementation of an assessment strategy for a new doctoral-level training programme for consultant clinical scientists.

John Gardner is a Professor of Education and Senior Deputy Principal of the University of Stirling, UK. His research interests include policy and practice in all sectors of education, particularly in relation to assessment. He has over 120 academic publications and has authored or co-authored seven books, including the most recent editorship of the four-volume *Assessment in Education* (2014). From 1994-2010, he was a member of the globally influential Assessment Reform Group, and he is currently a visiting professor at the Oxford University Centre for Educational Assessment. He is a fellow of the Chartered Institute of Educational Assessors and a fellow of the Academy of Social Sciences. In 2011, he completed a two-year term as President of the British Educational Research Association, and from 2011-2014 he was a member of the Education panel of the Research Excellence Framework, REF 2014.

Val Klenowski is Professor of Education at the Queensland University of Technology in Brisbane, Australia. Her research interests and publications are in the fields of curriculum change, evaluation, assessment, and learning. She has international recognition for her work on standards and moderation, classroom assessment, portfolio use for learning and assessment, equity, and assessment. She is the author of *Assessment for Education: Standards, Judgement and Moderation* (with Claire Wyatt-Smith, 2013).

Warwick Mansell is a freelance education journalist and author of the book *Education by Numbers: The Tyranny of Testing* (2007). Among his specialisms are assessment, the interaction of assessment with school accountability, and the interpretation of assessment data by policy-makers and the media. He spent nine years as a reporter with the *Times Educational Supplement*, the last six of which were as its assessment and curriculum correspondent. He now writes frequently for the *Guardian* newspaper.

Roger Murphy is Director of the Visual Learning Lab at the University of Nottingham, UK. His areas of interest and experience include educational research, evaluation, and assessment. He has a strong interest in educational innovations, which open up new ways for people to learn effectively. From that starting point he has become increasingly interested in visual approaches to supporting learning. He is also a former President of the British Educational Research Association.

Paul E. Newton is the Research Chair of Ofqual, based in Coventry, UK. He has previously held positions as Professor of Educational Assessment at the Institute of Education, University of London, UK, and as Director of the Cambridge Assessment Network division. His conceptualisation that public assessment systems have too many (often conflicting) purposes has been quoted far and wide – including having a prominent place in reports from the House of Commons Select Committee on education.

Onora O'Neill is Chair of the UK Equality and Human Rights Commission and is a cross-bench peer in the House of Lords. She was Principal of Newnham College, University of Cambridge, UK, from 1992 to 2006, and holds the title of Honorary Professor of Philosophy, Emeritus, University of Cambridge. She has written extensively on ethics, trust, and justice throughout her academic career and is highly regarded as a specialist on political philosophy. She chaired the Nuffield Foundation from 1998 to 2010, and was President of the British Academy from 2005 to 2009.

Lucy Simpson is a Doctoral Student at the Graduate School of Education, University of Bristol, UK. She is also an Honorary Research Fellow at the Department of Education, University of Oxford, UK. Her research is concerned with defining and measuring trust in public examinations.

Introduction

John Gardner

University of Stirling, UK

In drawing together this special issue about the Public Understanding of Assessment, the contributors have been conscious of parallels that can be drawn with the established field of the Public Understanding of Science, which seeks to address the lack of science knowledge among the general public. The impact and meaningfulness of science in everyday life offers a common thread, which Jenkins (1994) highlighted as the importance of context and 'knowledge in action' (p. 603) rather than knowledge for its own sake. Perhaps the most important aspects of science education in an everyday sense are those that have direct implications for the individual or society, e.g. the environment or food safety. In a similar way, the papers collected here variously adopt Harlen's people-focused view that '... what is important for everyone using or affected by assessment is not the details of definition but some general ideas, particularly about the trade-off between accuracy and meaning in assessment and the match of methods to purpose' (1994, p. 8).

Assessment of educational achievement, whether by traditional examinations or by teachers in schools, attracts considerable public interest, particularly when it is associated with 'high stakes' outcomes such as university entry or selection for employment. The usual outcome for the individual examination candidate is to receive a 'result', generally a discrete score, mark or grade. Sometimes this will not chime with their or their teachers' expectations and doubts will creep in about the process of assessment that has arrived at this result. However, educational assessment is a process that is made up of many layers of complexity, which are not always evident to the general public, including teachers, students and parents, and which are not easily understood outside the expert assessment community. These layers may be organised in highly co-dependent relationships that take in such matters as reliability, validity, human judgment and errors, and the uses and interpretations of the various types of assessment. No-one could reasonably argue that the principles and often nuanced complexities of educational assessment should be core learning in public education but there is a growing realisation that trust in the UK assessment system is under some threat as the media and others tend to sensationalise or politicise any problems that arise in the annual diet of examinations. This collection of papers offers the first comprehensive overview of how the general public is considered to perceive and understand a wide variety of aspects of educational assessment, and how this understanding may be improved.

The volume opens with O'Neill's exploration of public trust in assessment results and argues that it is not sufficient to pursue reliable and valid forms of assessment. She contends that published evidence about assessment must be provided in intelligible forms for those who need to decide whether or not to trust that evidence. This implies an intelligent form of accountability that can offer the general public a basis for placing or refusing trust in examinations (and in teachers and schools). Trust is also explored by Simpson and Baird, who report on how different stakeholders in the Advanced-level examinations process in England can have different expectations. They argue that many factors contribute to the generation of trust in examinations and that this makes it difficult to ensure that all of the stakeholders trust the system all of the time.

Klenowski's paper takes up the specific theme of trust in teacher's judgements, using the Australian experience of the impact of standards-based educational reforms. She argues that if the intention of assessment reforms is to improve educational outcomes rather than simply report them, then it is teachers that are the agents of change rather than the tests. As such, improved understanding of the value and process of teachers' judgement processes is a crucial focus in developing a public that is better informed about assessment.

Brookhart and Gardner both pick up the perception of objectivity underpinning much of the rhetoric around assessment scores. Brookhart, writing from a US perspective, recognises the problematics of objectivity but argues that, however much assessment experts may wish public understanding to be more appreciative of the nuances and complexities of assessment, the resulting scores provide a pragmatic means of absolving politicians, policymakers and the general public from any guilt in their interpretation or decision-making. She concludes that it may be more difficult to improve public understanding of the limits of assessment than to improve the quality of existing tests. Gardner also addresses the perceived objectivity of assessment, arguing that a misapprehension among the wider public that educational 'measurements' have scientific accuracy and precision has created the illusion of objectivity. Research suggests that instead of recognising the inevitability of various types of errors, the public tends to see them as avoidable mistakes by examination bodies or examiners. He sets out the challenge for the educational assessment community to choose their interactions carefully with the public, to wean them off the notions of accuracy and precision and to become more aware of the uncertainty implicit in assessment processes.

Several of the contributors tackle the nature and quality of existing communication processes. For example, Newton argues that reliability is a technical concept that has little real-world significance, preferring to tackle the more relevant and easier understood concept of 'measurement inaccuracy'. He suggests that the educational assessment community should use what he perceives as the language of media reporting, by referring to the likelihood of students getting the wrong grades. His paper considers the threats to public confidence in examinations and suggests that educational assessors should more specifically address the culpability for inaccuracy from the perspective of its causes and impacts. Chamberlain continues the communication theme for improved understanding of assessment processes among the users of examinations results, for example students, universities, employers and parents. She draws her contribution from other fields that share the characteristics of assessment, namely high public interest but ill-informed public understanding, and factual and technical complexity. The strategies she proposes for improving public understanding include focusing on the application of assessment information and recruiting influential peers as information brokers.

Communicating assessment matters in the media is the theme of the papers from both Mansell and Murphy, from the complementary perspectives of the journalist (Mansell) and the academic (Murphy). Mansell sets out evidence that suggests that at best there is misleading and at worst wilful mis-interpretation of public assessment data by the media and by politicians. He makes a plea for better mediation of the concept of uncertainty in assessment and also for greater engagement between the assessment community and the media. Murphy echoes the calls for better communication and media strategies from examination bodies, including making the key issues more accessible to the public, through utilisation of social networking to tap more effectively into the concerns of individuals, and encouraging the media to become better informed in their reporting.

The papers collectively highlight that there is much work to be done to ensure public confidence in educational assessment. In conclusion, it is important to endorse another tenet from the field of the Public Understanding of Science as a guiding principle. In seeking to improve the public understanding of assessment we must not '… imply a condescending assumption that any difficulties in the relationship between science [cf. the assessment community] and society are due entirely to ignorance and misunderstanding on the part of the public' (House of Lords, 2000, para 3.9). The onus is very much on the assessment community to improve how they mediate the various processes and outcomes.

References

Harlen, W. (1994). Developing public understanding of education: a role for educational researchers. *British Educational Research Journal*, 20(1), 3–16.

House of Lords (2000, 23 February). *Third report of the Select Committee on Science and Technology*. London, House of Lords. Available online at: http://www.parliament.the-stationery-office.co.uk/pa/ld199900/ldselect/ldsctech/38/3801.htm.

Jenkins, E. W. (1994). Public understanding of science and science education for action. *Journal of Curriculum Studies*, 26(6), 601–611.

Intelligent accountability in education

Onora O'Neill

House of Lords, London, UK

Systems of accountability are *second order* ways of using evidence of the standard to which *first order* tasks are carried out for a great variety of purposes. However, more accountability is not always better, and processes of holding to account can impose high costs without securing substantial benefits. At their worst, they may damage performance of the very first order tasks for which they supposedly improve accountability. In education this may happen if the assessment tail starts to wag the education dog. Teachers and learners, like others, need to be held to account, but this requires intelligent systems of accountability that do not distort primary activities. Intelligent accountability in education, as elsewhere, also needs to communicate, not merely to disseminate, relevant evidence that can be assessed by those to whom professionals and institutions are accountable.

Uses of assessment evidence

The evidence provided by systems of assessment can be used for many purposes. In schooling its most obvious and primary uses are educational: the results of pupil assessment can be used by pupils, parents and teachers to judge what has been learnt, to take appropriate educational steps, as well as to hold pupils to account for their learning—or lack of learning. However, the same evidence can also be reused to hold teachers and schools to account. Such secondary uses of assessment evidence may seem simple and convenient, but in fact lead to many complexities and difficulties.

For present purposes I shall set the primary, educational uses of assessment evidence aside, in order to concentrate on its reuse within the education system to assess a wider range of agents and institutions, and in particular to hold them to account. So I shall say little about the numerous uses of pupil assessments that bear on decisions made by or for individual pupils. My reason for bracketing these uses of educational assessment is not because they are unimportant: information

4

provided by educational assessment is used by pupils, their parents and others in making significant educational and employment choices. Pupils may be offered or refused coveted opportunities for further study or employment on the basis of assessment evidence of what they have or have not learnt. In itself, a favourable assessment is just that, but once linked to valued opportunities it becomes much more. In itself, an unfavourable assessment is just that: but when it becomes a basis for exclusion from valued education, training, employment or promotion it becomes much more. These familiar further uses of evidence provided by educational assessment are often of great importance, and in many cases life chances are at stake.

Life chances may also be at stake when the evidence provided by educational assessment is used for purposes that do not immediately bear on the prospects of individual pupils. When parents use school league tables as a basis for choosing a school, or for deciding to take on the expense of independent schooling, the stakes are high. And when poorly performing schools are faced with special measures, or closed—or not closed— life chances for pupils and staff may once again be at stake. In such cases the evidence provided by educational assessment is used to judge not those who have learnt (or failed to do so) but those who have taught or prepared them (or failed to do so), and so for holding teachers and schools to account.

Life chances are also at stake when evidence of pupil performance is used for still more remote purposes, such as supporting policy arguments for more, or better, or different sorts of education or training, or showing that we are doing enough to 'build a knowledge economy' or to survive the rigours of international competition— or alternatively that we are not. However, I shall say nothing about these more remote, though once again important, ways of reusing the evidence provided by educational assessment.

Goodhart's law and perverse incentives

Any claim that evidence provided by systems of assessment can be used to hold to account not only those who are assessed, but those who prepared them for assessment, deserves close scrutiny. The scrutiny is needed in order to take account of the ways in which the prospect of being held to account for others' performance, as measured by a given system of assessment, is likely to affect the action of those who do the preparation. While the hope of those who reuse assessment evidence for second-order purposes is that those who teach pupils and prepare them for examination will do it to a higher standard, the reality may be different. Teachers and schools may respond to such systems of accountability in ways that can undermine the very performance that is ostensibly being measured or assessed. Where this happens, the secondary use of assessment evidence to hold teachers and schools to account can damage primary, educational use of that assessment.

This sort of perverse effect of systems of accountability is sometimes referred to as an instance of 'Goodhart's law'. Charles Goodhart first articulated this law in a discussion of monetary policy, pointing out that 'Any observed statistical regularity will tend to collapse once pressure is placed upon it for control purposes' (Goodhart, 1984, p. 96). The problem has since been widely referred to in discussions of accountability, and especially of accountability in education. Marilyn Strathern, writing about university league tables, offered a formulation of Goodhart's law that is particularly apt as a warning about reusing educational metrics in order to hold third parties to account. Her formulation runs 'when a measure becomes a target it ceases to be a good measure' (Strathern, 1997, p. 308). Since then university league tables have proliferated and have been globalised, and universities see their rankings as a serious matter, to which they must attend closely if they are to recruit good students and staff.

These perverse effects of secondary uses of assessment evidence are, of course, not confined to banking or to university education. An even more prominent example is the widespread use in the UK of evidence obtained by pupil assessment to hold schools to account. The system of examination assessment generates ostensibly numerical scores for each pupil, which makes it possible to rank schools on the basis of the scores obtained by their pupils. These rankings are compiled by counting the number of 'passes', or so-called 'good passes' or 'points' that each pupil is awarded at GCSE, AS or A-level. These scores can then also be used to work out the *average* number of points per pupil, or the *average* number of A*–C marks per pupil, for a given school, or region, or type of pupil. These average scores and the league tables that are based on them can then, it is assumed, be used to hold teachers and schools to account.

However, these scores often do not provide good information about educational attainment or achievement, for several reasons. In the first place, neither the individual nor the average scores are more than *ostensibly* numerical. The ways in which a mark of 'A' or 'B' may be obtained vary, and the 'A' (or 'B', or 'C') obtained in one subject may not be educationally equivalent (whatever that means) to an 'A' (or 'B', or 'C') obtained in another subject. And when other qualifications are treated as 'equivalent' to GCSEs, the very idea that we are dealing with equivalent quantities is stretched to breaking point and beyond. A prime example is illustrated in Alison Wolf's recent report to the Department for Education (Wolf, 2011). Since the publication of this devastating report a range of vocational qualifications that were shown to provide little of value have been removed and their supposed equivalence to GCSE passes is no longer assumed. If we cannot show—and have no reason to assume—that examination point scores are accurate measures of educational attainment, it is hard to see what the rationale is for using these scores (as opposed to a more searching or relevant range of evidence of pupil attainment or capability) as a basis for admission to university or further training, or as a qualification for specific sorts of employment, let alone as evidence for holding teachers and schools to account. There is no genuine unit of educational achievement, as opposed to number of exam passes. Still, points are counted, though only up to a point: for many years universities were not told the numerical scores within the 'A' band. This made exam results uninformative for highly selective institutions.

However, given that choice of subject (apart from limited core requirements at GCSE level) is left to pupils as advised by schools, the arrays of scores achieved by different pupils in academic subjects are also not readily comparable. The fact that in England pupils are left to choose their options in the light of school provision and advice, and their own preferences, has profound effects. The absence of a unit of account might matter less if those applying for university admission had studied a common curriculum, since a rank ordering of pupil performances (as used in the USA) would then offer some support for discriminating judgement of performance that was relevant for allocating what is, after all, a positional good. However, work in the final two years of schooling in the UK is not defined by any common curriculum—and even in the previous two years there is considerable choice. Some of the deeper educational and other consequences of this 'choice agenda' can be seen in the apparently low levels of mathematical and reading attainment of pupils in the UK (and especially English pupils), compared to that of pupils in other school systems in developed countries. For example, the OECD *Programme for International Student Assessment* (PISA) shows the UK dropping down the rankings of pupil achievement in reading and mathematics in developed economies since 2000. However, PISA may not provide adequate comparisons for a range of reasons, such as those put forward by Jerrim (2011) and Foley and Goldstein (2012). The introduction of the e-Bac may reduce the problems above by creating an incentive to choose more academic subjects.

Universities that admit selectively try to compensate for the fact that this system of assessment neither ranks pupils adequately nor discriminates suitability for further study. Some universities do a little to call into question the arithmetic fiction that assigns the same weight to an 'A' in all subjects. They may discount A-levels in General Studies, or emphasise certain subjects as required or desirable for certain courses (however, this line of action is constrained by the fact that universities are required to show that they support 'access' for pupils of all backgrounds, even if they have chosen subjects that are not optimal for the university courses to which they aspire). Some take particularly serious account of GCSE marks, which are obtained before pupils are allowed to drop too many educationally fundamental subjects, so that there is a larger element of common curriculum and (arguably) a better basis for ranking students. Some use aptitude tests to augment the incomplete basis for judgement that A-level point scores offer them. Some employers make moves to check literacy and numeracy skills, which they fear GCSE will not have measured well. However, in the UK reservations about meritocracy are widespread, and demands for 'access' are often construed not as demands that attainments be fairly recognised, but as demands that admissions reflect social background proportionately.

The use of A-level passes or numbers of A*–C marks at GCSE as a basis for judging pupils who have chosen different options creates difficulties for university admissions. Where pupils have a choice of options there will be incentives for them—as also for parents and schools—to select subjects where good grades are actually or supposedly easier to come by, and to avoid subjects where they are actually or supposedly harder to obtain. Precisely *because* point scores at A-level, or the number of A*–C s at GCSE, matter for pupils and institutions under current conventions—*because* these elements of assessment form the basis for holding both to account—there is a strong incentive to choose subjects where higher numbers of points are expected more confidently, and to avoid subjects where they are thought harder to get. This can lead pupils to avoid subjects that are educationally important, including subjects that are needed for the university courses they aspire to. The results can be perverse.

Educationally perverse effects can be seen clearly in the steady and continuing decline in GCSE entries in modern languages, which have approximately halved in less than a decade. This huge decline in language teaching in maintained schools was triggered when the subject was made optional at GCSE, so no longer mattered for school accountability. There are now secondary schools in England that enter *no* pupils for *any* GCSE in *any* modern foreign language, with seeming unconcern about damaging their pupils' prospects. And many other schools have reduced both the number of GCSE entries in foreign languages, and the range of languages they offer, doing similar educational damage, to a lesser fraction of their pupils. This remarkable piece of educational vandalism was imposed in the name of increasing pupil choice in 2003–04, while Estelle Morris was Secretary of State.

This has happened for a range of reasons. In part it may reflect the fact that languages are reckoned by some to be more difficult than some other subjects, and by others to suffer from marking that is more erratic and more severe: if either is true, this shows that the supposed equivalence of GCSE marks in different subjects does not hold, and that systems of accountability that treat them as equivalent are based on poor metrics. However, the immediate trigger for the change was the decision to make languages optional regardless of the educational importance of language competence for a trading nation. The UK consequently now has less school language teaching than other European countries.

The fact that the system of accountability creates incentives for pupils and institutions to gravitate to subjects where adequate or good scores or points are perceived as more readily available shows that second-order uses of the outcomes of assessment for purposes of accountability can have adverse, indeed perverse, educational effects. Similarly, where HEIs and employers adjust recruitment to compensate for the fact that many pupils self-select out of subjects which are valuable for employment or university courses, even if they might have done well and gained educationally by making different choices, the incentives created by using assessment outcomes for accountability can damage central educational objectives. What starts as a perverse effect—the displacement of pupils into courses that are less educationally desirable for them—may soon become entrenched even for those who would have made better choices. For example, once the numbers of pupils taking a less favoured subject decline, provision can be cut back, and it may then become wholly rational to avoid those subjects. UK language education in schools at least provides a strikingly clear example of the accountability tail wagging the educational dog.

Accountability cannot replace trust

But what is the alternative? Should we revert from a culture of accountability based on objective assessment of performance to one in which we simply trust schools to ensure that pupils are coming along well, trust universities to admit the right students and trust employers to run fair appointments processes? During the last 25 years accountability has been widely seen as a *successor* to trust, and is now deeply entrenched in nearly all aspects of educational and professional life—and far beyond. The regulatory revolution that has transformed British life, and in particular the formerly nationalised industries and the public sector, including maintained schools, has reduced reliance on trust. Similar, if less drastic, changes have taken place in many other societies.

However, the assumption that accountability is an *alternative* to relations of trust is, I believe, mistaken both in and beyond education. The mistake has, I suggest, been based on widespread but unconvincing assumptions about the nature of trust. The central misleading assumption about trust is to see it as a generic attitude that provides a sort of cultural glue that provides 'social capital' in high-trust societies, which is missing or damaged in low-trust societies (for further reading on this issue, see Fukuyama, 1995, especially chapter 2 'The idea of trust'; and Putnam, 1995, 2000). On this view, trust once squandered is hard to restore, and little can be done to reverse the transition to low-trust societies. Trust is based on social habits rather than evidence about individual performance, and low-trust societies can do no better than replace trust with accountability. They are driven (to quote Francis Fukuyama) to 'co-operating only under a system of formal rules and regulations, which have to be negotiated, agreed to, litigated, and enforced, sometimes by coercive means' (Fukuyama, 1995, p. 27). Once trust is dissipated, or supposedly dissipated, it seems that the *only way* in which we can support co-operation is by imposing formal systems of accountability—despite the fact that such systems impose large transaction costs on all economic, not to mention educational, activity and create both damaging and perverse incentives. On this view, systems of accountability are seen as *replacing* trust by supporting trustworthy performance, thereby making it less important to judge where trust should be placed or refused. The restoration of trust is undesirable and pointless since the institutions of civil society on which it formerly depended have been eroded or discredited.

This view of trust as a matter of culture and attitude has been widely adopted during the last 15 years. For example, it is presupposed by the relentless use of opinion polls that assume that trust is merely a *generic* attitude which people have or lack. Pollsters ask their respondents undifferentiated questions, for example whether they trust those holding certain types of roles—doctors, teachers or journalists. Such questions assume that there can be no basis for an intelligent judgement about where to place and where to refuse trust. Any intelligent person would normally say that they trust some but not others holding these roles, and that they trust them in some matters but not in others. However, the assumption that trust is a free floating generic attitude, a miraculous bonding, binding cultural glue, licenses the thought that each person will assign a definite level of trust to *types* of office holders, without relying on or judging any specific evidence. In effect, respondents are asked to respond *on the assumption that all trust is blind trust*: any basis for differentiating cases, of the sort that we actually rely on in daily and professional life, is simply assumed away. Those who start with this view of trust unsurprisingly can find little to say in its favour. They tend to depict it as an infantile attitude, as evidence of dependence, and as something that has no proper place in the public life of mature democracy,

The claim that trust is obsolete in social and professional life, hence to be rejected in favour of accountability, could not, however, be further from the truth. We cannot have *any* form of accountability without *some* forms of trust. Those who recommend the increased oversight, monitoring of standards, recording of performance outcomes, sanctioning of poor performance and tighter contractual relations required by various contemporary forms of accountability have not miraculously discovered forms of accountability that work without trust. Rather they invite us to trust both certain complex, indeed arcane, processes of monitoring, inspecting and controlling that are introduced in the name of accountability, and those who impose them. Trust-free accountability is a mirage. We should not be surprised that replacing trust with accountability, life world with systems world, only pushes the question of where to place and where to refuse trust further back. We need to ask of any system of accountability why it should—or should not—be trusted. The various systems of accountability that use the outcomes of educational assessment as supposed metrics are no exception. We need to ask whether and when we have reason to trust them.

This point I think throws considerable light on the fact that there are few signs of any end to the supposed crisis of trust. The favoured, if ill-chosen, remedy for this supposed crisis has typically been a misguided attempt to supersede trust, rather than an effort to provide more useful evidence for placing and refusing trust intelligently. It has introduced massively complex systems of accountability, by which pupils, professionals, and the schools and colleges in which they work, are now controlled (see Power, 1997; Moran, 2003; and for parallel considerations in the case of education in the UK, see Mansell, 2007). However, since these systems of accountability are themselves of high complexity, even obscurity, they unsurprisingly fail to command public trust. Yet if they are not trusted they will not meet with public acceptance. In education, as elsewhere, over-complex systems of accountability, and in particular systems that create perverse incentives and frustrate serious educational objectives, are often a source rather than a remedy for mistrust.

Trust in assessment

Perhaps, however, we can be more optimistic about educational assessment and the forms of accountability for which it is reused than we can about other forms of assessment and accountability. After all, each of us has been at school and taken exams, and understands the primary uses of educational assessment. Should not reuses of the same evidence by systems of accountability be easier for most of us to understand than those that are used for holding insurers or bankers or broadcasters to account? So we might hope.

However, there are also reasons for being less optimistic. Many of us do not in fact understand how exams are marked, or what those who mark them aim to measure, or why the exams do not offer better evidence for selection for university admission or for employment. Anybody who deals with university admissions will have had heart-breaking correspondence with pupils or their parents, who cannot understand that what they see as amazing performance (all those As!) has not met with success, and who may be unable to imagine any better performance. In such circumstances, some suspect—or insist—that there must have been prejudice or unfair discrimination: since the outcome of the process seems wrong, the process is not trusted.

This may seem a small and local problem arising because the UK did not permit universities to have full assessment information, with the effect that they had difficulty in making distinctions near the top of the range, and had to supplement evidence of exam results with evidence from aptitude tests and other sources for university admission. However, the problem is deeper. In my view it arises from an uneasy attempt to combine meritocratic standards (pupil achievement should be recognised) with a widespread preference for non-meritocratic forms of equality. Hence the tendency to demand that abler pupils distinguish themselves mainly by achieving *more* passes than are likely to be educationally valuable or compatible with a full school life. Able pupils are ground down by Stakhanovite demands for quantity rather than quality of performance, and their schools are given the incentive to insist that they do this because each good pass by a pupil is an additional good pass for the school.

The combination of assessment and accountability that pupils face is widely seen as inflicting educational damage. Why then should we introduce more of the same? If pupils are *already* over-examined and *already* over-incentivised, and schools are *already* marginalising some educationally valuable activities for the sake of prettier exam profiles, what will be the effects of sharpening incentives yet further? Do we really want to increase the pressure for greater quantities of examination and assessment? Will not more of the same do further damage to education?

There are alternatives. One would be to make fuller evidence of comparative performance more public, for example by publishing an order of merit at 'A' level or indeed at GCSE. More selective universities in the USA do something close to this: their commitment to meritocracy is unequivocal, and they can access full rank-in-class information as well as detailed SAT scores. This route would probably be unpopular in the UK, because publishing more complete numerical information about pupil performance might not help those from disadvantaged backgrounds. Yet others would find it unacceptable if 'access' was secured by explicitly preventing universities from using meritocratic admissions criteria. For that would undermine the incentives that assessment systems create for and rely on in pupils and schools, and would be seen as unfair. There might even be litigation if some schools found that excellent performance was not rewarded for social reasons, as was the case in certain Eastern Europe countries under Communism, where children from bourgeois or dissident homes were straightforwardly barred from university study.

Although these two approaches would probably be seen as unacceptable in the UK, we need to consider how much educational damage are we already tolerating for the sake of a muddled approach to assessment and accountability. Quite apart from issues of university admissions, the examination system now diverts a lot of time that would once have been available for teaching to assessment, even to mock rehearsals for assessment, whose results are then fed to the accountability juggernaut: this is surely educationally damaging. In the end, it seems to me, no change in assessment methods or structures of accountability is acceptable if it causes educational damage, let alone creates perverse incentives. Assessment is *not* an end in itself. If we do not question the policies that base accountability for pupils, professionals and schools on pupil performance in assessment systems, we may forget that the primary purpose of school assessment is education.

Trust and accountability

These problems may, however, show less about systems of assessment than they show about conceptions of accountability that reuse the results of assessment. Although many of us think that we understand what school assessment is *for*—mainly for educational purposes and sometimes for selection purposes—we may be less aware and less confident about the further purposes for which the results of assessment are used. I had a startling illustration of this point after giving the Reith Lectures, when I was asked by a local journalist why I had been sceptical about the school league tables. I asked her what she thought their merit was, and was told that without them it would be impossible to be sure that one's children were at a better school than other people's children! It is easy to laugh at this reply, or to condemn it. But I think she may have got matters right, even if her way of putting it was not politically correct. League tables are (seemingly) easily understood *because* they offer a ranking, so provide a *seeming* basis for comparative judgements about the merits of different schools. Yet league tables will not reveal which are good and which are poor schools, let alone for which children. This emphasis on *comparative* measures is likely to appeal to those who care more about positional goods than about good education.

The simplified types of information about school performance that are derived ultimately from assessment evidence, and provided for public consumption, at least rank pupils. But they may not do much more. Ofsted reports are of course another matter, although perhaps not as informative as they might be. The types of information that are perused by professionals and examination boards are yet another matter. Yet it is the assessment evidence as compiled into league tables that is mainly offered to the public as evidence of the quality of schools.

It is hardly surprising that those who are invited to trust on the basis of this information feel that they are not well placed to assess what pupils and schools achieved and are reluctant to trust the very exams that pupils are urged to take, and retake, and take more of. Those who are invited to trust these systems of accountability know little about the underlying assumptions and limitations, or about the technicalities of assessment. Pupils, parents, teachers, schools and the general public know little about the statistical issues that make one or another aspect of assessment more or less reliable. They may have no sense of differences between reliability and validity; and may not know much about the merits and limits of the sorts of assessment in use. By contrast, they are likely to be aware of the importance of avoiding subjects in which it is said to be harder to get a good mark (e. g. languages, mathematics)—but not of the perverse effects on education and employment of opting out of learning mathematics and languages.

It is true that a great deal of information about schools and exams is made available to the public in the name of transparency; but transparency or disclosure is a far cry from adequate communication, and may not offer enough to those who have little time or expertise to enable them to place or refuse trust intelligently. Those of us who cannot make these judgements for ourselves will often be unable to judge whether to place or refuse trust in the relevant systems of assessment, or in the forms of accountability that reuse the evidence provided by those systems of assessment. In making these claims I am not assuming that current assessment practices are untrustworthy, or even that the forms of accountability that use them are untrustworthy (although I have argued that the latter are often perverse). However, it is evident that current systems of accountability are too complex for pupils, parents, or even teachers to judge them for themselves. Hence it is not reasonable to expect that they should be trusted.

Towards intelligent accountability

What would we have to achieve if we seek an examination system that is not only trustworthy, but one in which people can place and refuse trust with some confidence? As I see it, placing and refusing trust is not a matter of being mired in cultural glue, but of being able *to judge for oneself* what a pupil, a school or an education system is achieving. It is doubtful whether the copious evidence made available about *comparative* pupil performance on technically complex and sometimes educationally dubious metrics provides what is needed for the intelligent placing and refusal of trust.

Forms of assessment that can be judged by the inexpert are urgently needed. This is not the same as saying that reliable and valid forms of assessment are urgently needed. It is a matter of ensuring that the evidence about reliable and valid forms of assessment is provided in intelligible forms to those who need to decide whether or not to trust that evidence. An intelligent form of accountability would need to offer the public, parents and pupils evidence *which they can use* as a basis for placing or refusing trust in teachers, in exams and in schools. Such evidence would need to allow people to make informed judgements about where to place and where to refuse trust. It is not hard to suggest some changes that could help. I offer a few, quite brief, suggestions:

(1) Neither intelligent accountability nor public trust in systems of accountability is well served by holding schools or teachers accountable for scores on 'performance indicators' that use bogus units of measurement. Serious accountability is undermined rather than supported when teachers and schools are held to account by measures like 'number of A–C grades per pupil at GCSE', or 'average A-level point scores': serious professionals know that different exams make different demands, and that these composite scores are not genuinely comparable. Numbers are useful when we have a unit of account: we can count pupils, and we can count the money in school budgets. Many things that are important for education *cannot* be counted, or added, or ranked because there is no genuine unit of account.

(2) Bogus numbers are not just an expensive irrelevance. They also are a significant source of perverse incentives, such as incentives to avoid subjects that are demanding (but perhaps educationally important), incentives to invest disproportionate effort in pupils who might get 'Ds', or (at their saddest) incentives to 'massage' the 'statistics' of pupil achievement (e.g. by choosing the least demanding examination board or subject, and by 'teaching for the test') rather than by teaching those pupils better. They create incentives to enter abler pupils for excessive numbers of exams, so that the average score for a school is higher than it would otherwise be. When the scores are published, there is still no underlying unit of account and so only a poor basis for the pupils, their parents or the wider public to decide how much trust to place in a given exam result, or in a particular teacher or school. School league tables may tell parents that some school is 'better' or 'worse' than some other (local) school *as measured by the performance indicators*: but they don't even aim to show that school is a good school, let alone a good school for a particular child. As anybody can see, position in a league table is a *comparative* measure; in some cases it will be administratively useful, but by itself it does not guarantee quality—or lack of quality. In educating children, as in the rest of life, we often need to make serious judgements of quality as well as, or even in place of, relational judgements of success.

(3) Changing the performance indicators is not likely to resolve these problems. Yet faith in performance indicators is hard to dislodge. Every time one performance indicator is shown to be inaccurate, or misleading, or likely to produce perverse results, some people claim that they can devise a better one that has no perverse effects. Experience suggests that they may well be

as wrong as those who invented the last lot of indicators. Systems of assessment need to dance to the tune of educational objectives—not to the tune of accountability convenience.

(4) Change will be possible only if we are clear about educational aims. But if we retain the options-based approach to secondary education, combined with a fiction that treats scores on the assessments of different options as using a common unit of educational quality, then we will be tempted to continue to allow a certain approach to accountability to reuse the results of educational assessment, even if doing this damages education itself. Although there are cases in which it is rational to assume without evidence that all instances of a given class have the same weight or significance, it is not in the least plausible to assume that all instances of a given score at GCSE or at A-level have the same educational weight or significance. It is more than clear that no pupils, teachers, schools or universities *really* accept that a given A-level point score or a given number of A*–C passes has a uniform educational significance. They may talk about A-level points, or about numbers of A*–C passes at GCSE, when paying due deference to the dominant approaches to accountability. In practice they take for granted that different subjects make demands of varied difficulty, and that subjects will be chosen partly with this in mind. However, if systems of accountability artificially make it riskier to choose harder but educationally important subjects, some pupils, teachers and schools will go for options that are substantively less useful to them because they think—perhaps correctly—that these are likely to attract 'better' assessments, even if they produce educational detriment.

(5) If the options problem could be solved, and schools taught and pupils studied a common curriculum, there might over time be more public confidence in the results of educational assessment. Educational assessment does not have to be coupled with forms of accountability that create perverse incentives and damage educational objectives. It could be coupled with intelligent forms of accountability that aim at *informed* and *independent* judgement of the results of assessment, and communicate those judgements *intelligibly*. In fact, educational assessment offers a much better basis for intelligent accountability than is available in many other domains of life. It is, or at least it could be, assessment by people who are sufficiently *informed* to judge the performance they assess, sufficiently *independent* to do so objectively, and able and permitted to report *intelligibly* to the *various* audiences to whom an account is to be given. Such changes could offer a basis for a more intelligent approach to accountability, and a promising basis for the more intelligent placing and refusal of trust.

References

Foley, B. & Goldstein, H. (2012). *Measuring success: league tables in the public sector*, British Academy Policy Centre Report. Available online at: http://www.britac.ac.uk/policy/Measuring-success.cfm

Fukuyama, F. (1995). *Trust: the social virtues and the creation of prosperity*. New York, Free Press.

Goodhart, C. (1984). *Monetary theory and practice. the UK experience*. London, Macmillan.

Jerrim, J. (2011). *England's 'plummeting' PISA test scores between 2000 and 2009: is the performance of our secondary school pupils really in relative decline?* Department of Quantitative Social Science, Institute of Education. Available online at: http://www.ioe.ac.uk/Study_Departments/J_Jerrim_qsswp1109.pdf

Mansell, W. (2007). *Education by numbers: the tyranny of testing*. London, Politico's Publishing.

Moran, M. (2003). *The British regulatory state: high modernism and hyper-innovation*. Oxford, Oxford University Press.

Power, M. (1997). *The audit society: rituals of verification*. Oxford, Oxford University Press.

Putnam, R. (1995). Bowling alone: America's declining social capital. *The Journal of Democracy*, 6(1), 65–78.

Putnam, R. (2000). *Bowling alone: the collapse and revival of American community*. New York, Simon & Schuster.

Strathern, M. (1997). Improving ratings: audit in the British university system. *European Review*, 5, 305–321.

Wolf, A. (2011). *Review of vocational education* (the Wolf Report). Department for Education. Available online at: https://www.education.gov.uk/publications/standard/Post16Learning/Page1/DFE-00031-2011

Perceptions of trust in public examinations

Lucy Simpson[a] and Jo-Anne Baird[b]
[a]*University of Bristol, UK;* [b]*University of Oxford, UK*

Over recent years, the credibility of public examinations in England has increasingly come to the fore. Government agencies have invested time and money into researching public perceptions of the reliability and validity of examinations. Whilst such research overlaps into the conceptual domain of trust, trust in examinations remains an elusive concept. Little is known about what it *means* to trust in examinations and on what individuals base their trust judgments. This paper reports the findings of research into key stakeholders' perceptions of trust in the English A-level examination system through a series of focus groups comprising (separately) of examination board staff, students, higher education admissions tutors, teachers and the general public. Analysis of the data revealed a number of factors that are integral to the concept of trust in A-levels, including examination standards, the marking of examination papers, the syllabus, communication and provision of information, whether A-levels are fit for purpose and the mode of assessment. The fact stakeholders have different expectations and requirements of the A-level system, which are subject to change, means that it is difficult for the A-level system to engender the trust of all of its users all of the time.

Introduction

Trust is central to the credibility of examination systems. Examination results are a form of 'currency'—and like all currencies they must be trusted by their users to hold any meaning within a social system (Wiliam, 1996; Nisbet, 2007). In England, a major threat to trust in national examinations has been the news media's coverage of several aspects of the system. The publication of examination results in England has routinely been accompanied by headlines that educational standards are falling and that examinations are getting easier (Murphy, 2004). The procedures used by examination boards to grade and monitor students' work have also been subjected to scrutiny (Warmington & Murphy, 2004). A more recent scandal broke in December 2011, amidst claims from undercover reporters that examiners were 'cheating' by giving teachers confidential advice about how to achieve higher grades. Examination boards were accused of competing to win 'business' from schools, and of consequently driving down educational standards. The scandal followed the Education Secretary, Michael Gove, denouncing the examination system as 'discredited' and in need of fundamental reform (Watt *et al.*, 2011a, b, 2011b). Thus, politicians' positions in the media can form part of the threat to trust. At the time of writing, for the first time in England, a group of pupils, schools and councils are seeking a judicial review of the grading of examinations in English taken at age 16 (BBC, 2012). This is an indication of the level of mistrust more broadly in the examination system.

Given the controversy surrounding examinations in the national press, it is not surprising that examinations have increasingly attracted the government's attention. In 2008, legislation was passed to create the Office of the Qualifications and Examinations Regulator (Ofqual)—an independent watchdog charged with the task of improving public confidence. Research commissioned by the government into examinations has included a longitudinal survey of stakeholder's perceptions of examinations in general (Ipsos MORI, 2003a, 2003b, 2004, 2006a, 2006b, 2007, 2010, 2011, 2012), and perceptions of the reliability of results (Ipsos MORI, 2009; Chamberlain 2010; He *et al.*, 2010). Most recently, Ofqual has launched an investigation into the validity of assessments. The authors believe that whilst such research is relevant to the concept of trust—reliability and validity are likely to form part of trust in examinations—a more focused approach is needed to investigate trust itself. Commentary exclusively on trust in examinations has been anecdotal (Tate, 2005) or philosophical (O'Neill, 2005). Little is known about what it *means* to trust in examinations, on what individuals base their trust judgements, and what could be done to improve trust. For this reason, our research focuses upon the English context; it is a good place to start because it is an environment that we understand well and where high-stakes examinations have a high profile in society, the media and politics.

Notwithstanding the above, one area of social life where trust is well-researched is the medical profession. Whilst some researchers have been concerned with trust in the doctor–patient relationship (e.g. Anderson & Dedrick, 1990), others have examined trust in health-care systems (e.g. Straten *et al.*, 2002). In terms of the latter, tools to measure trust in health-care systems have been developed, which have enabled key determinants of trust to be identified (Calnan & Sanford, 2004). In addition, some commentators have suggested that such tools may be helpful in predicting patient behaviour e.g., consulting 'alternative practitioners' (Straten *et al.*, 2002). Whilst strong parallels exist between educational assessment and medical diagnosis (errors occur in both and are high-stakes—see Newton, 2005), the authors recognise that drawing inferences about trust in examinations based on research from the broader medical profession is more problematic. The authors argue, however, that research in the medical profession highlights some potential benefits of studying trust in the context of examinations. Definitions of trust are thought to be highly context dependent.

Where little is known about how trust functions, it is recommended that qualitative research be conducted to explore how respondents view trust and trusted behaviour (Goudge & Gilson, 2005). This paper reports on the findings of a qualitative study into perceptions of trust in A-level examinations. A-levels were chosen as the focus of inquiry because they are often referred to as the 'gold standard' of assessment and are students' main route to university, college or employment in England. The study is an initial exploration into trust in examinations, and was thus small in scale. The findings will be informative for a subsequent large-scale quantitative study, designed to *measure* trust in A-levels. Before discussing the study, a brief note on A-levels and the relevant agencies is necessary to understand the context of the study.

The A-level qualification

A-level stands for Advanced level. They are two-year, post-compulsory qualifications, typically sat by 16–18 year-olds in schools and colleges. The examinations currently have a modular structure, with some A-levels composed of four units and others six units. Assessment is largely by written examinations, although in some subjects there is a limited amount of coursework. Subjects such as science or art also include practical assessments. Grades are from A to E and most of the entrants (97.8% in 2011) gain at least a grade E because students who are unlikely to pass tend to drop out of a particular subject's examination. An additional A*
grade was made available at A-level only in 2010. It is possible for students to resit individual units to try to improve their overall grade. If schools or colleges suspect that something has gone awry with the marking of an examination paper, it is possible to request copies of marked scripts. There is also the facility to request a re-count or re-mark. If still dissatisfied, it is possible to appeal to Ofqual or the Independent Examinations Appeals Board.

In England, three main examination boards (also known as awarding bodies) offer A-levels: The Assessment and Qualifications Alliance (AQA), Edexcel and OCR (Oxford Cambridge and RSA Examinations). Students, or in practice, schools, are able to choose which syllabus and examination to take in each subject. Ofqual is responsible for regulating the examination boards. A-levels have an enormous weight of societal expectation placed upon them, as they are a vehicle of meritocracy for selection to Higher Education and employment. Naturally, therefore, there are also controversies surrounding them. We referred earlier to 2011 scandals regarding teacher training by examination boards, but there are other recurrent themes that form the backdrop to this study (Baird, 2009). As they arise in and are illustrated by the findings of the research, we do not outline them here. Before outlining the study, we briefly turn to what we mean by 'trust'.

What is trust?

The most common distinction made with respect to the definition of trust is that between 'interpersonal' trust and 'social trust', whereby only interpersonal trust involves face-to-face commitment, as opposed to 'faceless commitments' toward other social objects (Giddens, 1990; cited in Sztompka, 1999, p. 41). Sztompka (1999, p. 42) objects to this over-simplistic distinction; rather than a dichotomy, he conceives of trust as 'gradual, expanding, concentric circles' or 'radius of trust' starting with the most intimate personal relations towards more abstract social objects, such as institutions, technological systems and regimes. This conception of trust seems more satisfactory, since it is fluid and recognises that behind all social objects, such as the education system, there are people, and it is the people whom we ultimately bestow with trust. Our research has been framed with the following definition of trust as 'a bet about the future contingent actions of others' (Sztompka, 1999, p. 25).

Methodology

Participants

Six focus groups, with a total of 36 participants (14 male and 22 female) were conducted between May 2009 and December 2009. One focus group was conducted with each of the following groups; examination board staff, first-year undergraduate students, admissions tutors for Higher Education, and the general public. Two focus groups were convened with A-level teachers. The number and size of the focus groups was appropriate to the nature of the research as an initial probe into the un-researched area of trust in examinations.

The groups were selected because each was perceived to have a different relationship with the A-level examination system: examination board staff are involved in the development and delivery of A-levels; students have recent experience of studying for, and taking, their A-levels; teachers have experience of teaching A-level syllabuses, preparing students for A-level examinations, and being held accountable for results; admissions tutors rely on A-level results to help them discriminate amongst students for admittance to university courses. Although members of the general public do not have such an obvious stake in the A-level system, this group was included to gauge the perceptions of 'laypeople'.

Opportunity sampling was used to select participants for the study, although each group necessitated a slightly different recruitment strategy (Table 1). Examination board staff were recruited from an English examination board. Senior managers from across the organisation were contacted via email and asked to recruit two volunteers from within their department to participate in a focus group. Students, teachers and admissions tutors were all recruited from the North-West of England. Specifically, first-year undergraduate students were recruited via advertisements posted on university careers websites. Admissions tutors were contacted directly to

Table 1. Focus group participants and recruitment strategy

	No. of focus groups	Males	Females	Recruitment strategy
Examination board staff	1	3	3	Via senior manager
Students	1	3	3	Advertisement on careers website
Admissions tutors	1	2	2	Direct via email or telephone
General public	1	4	4	Via community liaison officer at a corporate company
Teachers	2	2	10	Via headteachers
Total	6	14	22	

ask whether they would be willing to participate in a focus group exploring trust in A-levels. Likewise, head teachers were contacted to ask whether A-level teachers in their school would be interested in taking part in the study. A selective secondary school and a sixth-form college were recruited—one focus group was held with teachers in each. Finally, a large corporate company was approached to recruit members of the general public. The company is a national energy supplier, with a strong sense of corporate responsibility. Education represents a key area of the company's community programme, which is why the company readily offered its support. A member of the company's Community Team acted as a liaison whilst negotiating, recruiting for, and conducting the focus group.

Focus group format

Focus groups lasted between one and a half and two hours and were led by the same researcher. Each session was opened with an introduction, a statement of the overall purpose of the research, and an explanation of the ground rules—for instance, participants were asked not to talk over each other (Finch & Lewis, 2003). Next, participants were split into two groups and asked to complete a warm-up exercise, lasting approximately 20 minutes. Specifically, participants were asked to think about 1) the attributes that a trustworthy person has and 2) a company or institution that they particularly distrust and their reasons. Each sub-group recorded their responses on flipcharts. The warm-up exercise was intended to foster thinking about the abstract concept of trust and to help build a rapport amongst participants.

The remainder of the session took the form of a group discussion. Participants were asked to describe past experiences that had led them to trust in the A-level system, and past experiences that had caused them to lose, or not establish trust. The session also included a discussion of the media's impact on trust in A-levels, and what organisations like examination regulatory bodies could do to help engender trust. In each focus group, the role of the researcher was to encourage comments from all participants (e.g. asking 'what does everyone else think?'), to guide the discussion back to the central issue of trust in A-levels, and to ask for clarification or expansion on comments (Krueger & Casey, 2000). The discussions flowed freely and required relatively little intervention by the researcher. An observer was also present at each session to take field notes regarding the mood, non-verbal communication, and the order that participants spoke in to aid later transcription (Parker & Tritter, 2006).

Each session was audio-recorded and transcribed verbatim. At the beginning of the focus group, participants signed a consent form giving their permission for the data they supplied to be audio-recorded, transcribed and analysed. Participants were also made aware of the ethical protocol; all the data would be made anonymous, specific individuals would not be identified in resultant reports, and they could withdraw from the research at any time.

Data analysis

The focus groups generated qualitative data totalling nearly 60,000 words. Due to the teacher focus groups being conducted at a slightly later date, the analysis was conducted in two stages. In the first stage, the transcripts from the focus groups with examination board staff, students, admissions tutors and the general public were analysed using content analysis (Spencer *et al.*, 2003). The transcripts were read several times to allow the initial identification of themes and later analysed using the qualitative software package, NVivo. Once the initial coding process had been conducted, a second researcher independently reviewed clean copies of the transcripts. The task of the second researcher was not to code all of the data, but simply to identify key themes. Similar themes emerged from the initial coding process and the independent review of the transcripts.

In the second stage, the transcripts from the teacher focus groups were analysed for any new emergent themes. The data were coded and integrated into the initial data set, using NVivo. The inclusion of the teacher focus group data increased the importance of communication and provision of information as a theme. Teachers also introduced issues concerning online marking and the development and support of syllabuses. Multiple coding of all of the data is prohibitively resource-intensive, but the discussions arising from the checking of the key themes in the first stage of this coding process was sufficient to clarify and consolidate the main codes arising from the data (Barbour, 2001).

Findings

Content analysis of the qualitative data revealed six dominant themes in terms of participants' perceptions of trust in A-level examinations. Each theme is outlined below, along with illustrative quotations.

Examination standards

Examination standards represented one of the most dominant themes in the group discussions. Teachers and the general public, in particular, were concerned with the issue of the maintenance of examination standards over time. Despite claims that standards are falling being commonplace in the British press, there was disagreement within each group about whether A-levels are getting easier, with some participants attributing higher pass rates to improvements in the quality of teaching:

> I talk to loads of people from time to time, including someone I'm still in touch with from the first school I taught at and left about twenty years ago ... and we're absolutely convinced that the sort of quality of the exam papers and the expectations on the students has decreased you know, you might call it dumbing down. (Geography teacher)

> I think I would disagree with you as far as Classics is concerned ... the skills which are being demanded of them are greater than were demanded of me when I did my A-levels ... the questions are very demanding in terms of, particularly A2, with synopticity, the skills that they require to answer those questions are tremendous. (Classics teacher)

Another sub-theme was the comparability of inter-board standards. Participants from across all groups recognised the importance of comparability between the different examination boards in terms of the quantity and quality of work expected of students and the final grades awarded. A number of participants suggested that a single examination board would be fairer and more trustworthy:

> if we keep going back to this business of trust in the A-level system ... we're talking about making sure that you know, A's, B's, C's, D's ... are the same between the exam boards, so that universities, for example, know that candidates coming through Edexcel are a similar standard if they got an A than you know candidates coming out of AQA ... for example. (Geography teacher)

> I think just the fact ... there are a number of awarding bodies shows that there's a problem because the difference between what one awarding body would kind of set as a curriculum and then mark is different to another ... And I actually think that's fundamentally at the root of the problem, it's that you haven't got a consistent approach. You should have one awarding body surely so that it's fair. (General public)

Participants recognised the perverse educational effects that differential standards between boards may bring about; with schools and teachers potentially favouring certain examination boards over others because they offer an easy option and are likely to award better grades, rather than basing their decision solely on the educational value of the syllabus:

> I think the schools have probably picked the awarding body that provides either the easiest [syllabus] for their staff to teach or the easiest for exams or assessment, so that their school looks good because they'll get good grades. (General public)

The general public and teachers were not only concerned with inter-board comparability, but also inter-subject comparability. Both groups indicated awareness that A-level grades in some subjects are valued more than others. Such assertions imply that all A-levels are not viewed as equal; individuals may place greater trust in the information provided by examinations in traditional subjects than less traditional subjects:

> The core ones [A-levels] aren't easier and people are thinking that when someone says 'I've got five As', I don't think people just say like 'aw brilliant', I think they are like 'oh what did you take?' And then I think that gives the different like reaction if you say Maths, Physics, Chemistry, French and Biology or if you said like Media and Drama. (General public)

Marking

The marking of examination papers and moderation of coursework also proved to be central to participants' perceptions of trust in the A-level examination system. Students and teachers, more so than the other groups, were concerned about the reliability or consistency of marking. Many of the participants drew upon personal experiences, or experiences of friends or family, to describe situations where marking had been found to be erroneous. These experiences undermined trust in A-levels, and national examinations more generally. Emotions ran high when participants discussed cases where marking had gone awry; there was a strong sense that, due to the high-stakes nature of national examinations for students, teachers and schools, mistakes were inexcusable. Furthermore, participants viewed the facility offered by examination boards to request a re-mark negatively. The fact that re-marks can, and do, happen seemed to undermine their trust. The following quotes below illustrate their thoughts on marking reliability:

> There have been times in the past where for one particular section of a paper ... I'm talking about English... that whole section we felt has been completely mismarked. You know, we've had to send things back, and that as you say, that one incident then makes you lose trust in the rest of it and then you start to feel, and it's coming back to consistency isn't it? You feel like 'how well are these papers being checked, moderated, and what is the standard of these examiners?' So sometimes, some years I've had a lot of trust in them [A-levels] and then other years that trust has been lost. (English teacher)

> The fact that you have the opportunity to get it re-marked kind of gives the idea that maybe it's not marked correctly. (Student)

Teachers also suggested that the introduction of online marking may introduce further inconsistency into the system. They felt that it may be difficult to accurately mark essays and coursework onscreen, and that the use of new technology may lead to the attrition of some of the most experienced examiners:

> a lot of things are going to be marked online and I have severe doubts about whether you can mark essay subjects effectively online. And that may well change my perception and may well change my idea of trust. I know that there are, with one board, where things that have gone online, there are more issues with re-marks. (Classics teacher)

> from their [examiners] point of view, you have to have an up to date computer to be actually able to use, access the different systems. So unless you're actually prepared to buy yourself a new computer, in certain instances, then you are actually going to lose really experienced people, which is not good. (Art and technology teacher)

Finally, students and teachers discussed marking reliability at the level of the examiner. Students suggested that factors such as examiner fatigue may influence the final mark a student received. Students also questioned the motives of examiners, suggesting that they may mark papers quickly for monetary gain and may not have students' best interest at heart. Teachers were concerned that inexperienced and poor examiners may not fully understand the material they are marking and introduce inconsistency into the system:

> The more they [examiners] do the more money they get the quicker they mark the more money they get, less time they have to spend on it. So, it's in their nature to mark quickly, do it quickly, not rush but 'hey if I can finish this in an hour maybe I can do a few more, make a few more pounds' and the teachers aren't the highest paid so why not? But to them it's just a tick tick tick and give a mark which to somebody else is you know their A-levels, it's their future .... (Student)

> members of the department who do go to the boards are very concerned about the quality of some of the other markers ... because you can clearly see at the examiners' meeting that they actually don't understand the material that they're going to be marking on. So, we have experiences of students writing a perfect answer, but it looks just slightly different from the marking scheme, even though it's completely equivalent' and getting no marks at all on the papers that come back. (Mathematics teacher)

The syllabus

All groups, with the exception of the general public, touched upon issues relating to the syllabus when discussing their trust in A-levels. With regard to the question papers used to test the syllabus, participants felt that a coherent link between the two was paramount. Notably, examination board staff seemed to feel that A-level question papers were fair, whilst students tended to be distrustful of question papers, suggesting that they had been designed to 'trick' or deceive them:

> I would generally think the question papers I've seen are fair, in the sense that they don't, very clearly, advantage a group of candidates that are coming from one particular perspective, compared to another. (Examination board staff)

> I think if they're [examiners] trying to deceive you, like make you think that they're asking about one thing when they're actually asking you about something in a round-about way, you'd rather they be to the point and then I think that's a trust thing really. (Student)

Furthermore, the students suggested that the way a question is phrased or worded can sometimes unfairly impact upon a student's ability to provide a response. Here, the students were touching upon the important issue of question validity; a poorly worded question may not provide a valid measure of a student's ability or knowledge in a certain area:

> People's understanding of like the way things are worded isn't as good as other people, so one person might understand that straight away and the other person could be like 'oh my god, what does that mean?', and they could know even more than the person who understood the question. (Student)

Admissions tutors, in particular, felt that the content of A-levels was important to students, teachers, and universities and employers looking to take on students post-A-level. However, one admissions tutor suggested that whilst A-levels may not cover all of the material he would like, this was something fundamentally different to trust. He made the following comment:

> Somehow the design of them [A-levels] or content of them isn't really what we need or what we want it to be. Which is different to saying we don't trust them. (Mathematics admissions tutor)

In their discussions, teachers focused upon the guidance and support they received from examination boards in helping them to teach A-level syllabuses. Effective training which helps teachers to interpret the syllabus and gauge what is expected of their students was essential for teachers. In addition, teachers valued the provision of high-quality resources, such as textbooks written by the Chief examiner, to assist them in their teaching. Finally, there was evidence to suggest that consulting teachers during the development of new syllabuses serves to increase their trust in the end result:

> I was quite impressed with the way that AQA in particular handled the new specifications for GCSE ... I felt that they talked to teachers more before making their decisions and I really felt that did improve my trust and I felt that when I went to a series of meetings, each time they'd been to talk to different focus groups, for instance, and actually you could see they'd made amendments to what they'd intended to do, so I do think that that's important, to get feedback from the people who are actually going to be teaching. (English teacher)

Communication and provision of information

For teachers only, communication with examination boards was central to their conception of trust in the broader A-level system. Specifically, teachers made reference to telephone dealings they had had with examination board staff. Teachers often contact examination boards at highly pressured times, such as shortly before an examination or on the receipt of A-level results, to seek support and guidance. At these times, teachers valued a personalised, professional and efficient response to their queries. Standardised responses, lacking in consideration for their individual circumstances, seemed to disappoint and frustrate them:

> I find when I ring up I frequently get someone who will just appear to read from a card 'oh put them in for re-marking'... I know about re-marks ... I could write the book on remarks ... I finally found one person this year who was a head of section who ... was the first person who spoke sense to me ... but all I ever get is the kind of 'this is what you have to do'. There's never any kind of sense of somebody thinking about you as a centre, you know, you as a head of subject or whatever it is ... you with a particular set of students whose marks are way out of what you were expecting or way out of what they got the last time. You know, all you ever get is the kind of party line. (English teacher)

A more prevalent theme concerned the provision of information about examination boards and their regulators and the processes used to award examinations. Some participants expressed confusion about the different examination boards and regulators that exist, and what they are responsible for. Overly frequent changes to the structures that support the A-level system seemed, in part, to be responsible for this confusion:

> Do they [educationalists] know what they're doing because you know, you've got QCDA and every time I seem to turn around there's another board or they've divided into something else and nobody really seems to know what their individual responsibilities are ... (Classics teacher)

Others showed a desire for greater information about standard-setting processes, as well as data about examination results. Discussions amongst participants seemed to suggest that wider availability of such information would enable examination users to make informed judgements about whether or not to place trust in the system:

> we need from somebody, the right sort of data that enables us to make comparisons between boards and between subjects that is accurate and valid data. (Geography teacher)

Although, perhaps understandably, examination board staff seemed reticent about disclosing too much information about standard-setting processes and examination data, suggesting that in the wrong hands it could easily be misinterpreted, leading to a breakdown in trust. One participant's recollection of a discussion with colleagues about whether or not journalists should be invited to observe standard-setting meetings demonstrates this point:

> I remember, we had, a conversation once, with a number of people in the board about whether we should invite journalists into awarding [standard-setting] meetings, and there were very clearly two camps. People who were saying 'absolutely, total transparency, it would be really helpful', and others who were saying 'journalists will never understand it, all they'll see are two examiners who are talking about the real margins of where a grade is, and not coming into complete agreement, and they'll run with that, you know, they can't even agree marks amongst themselves, how can we be confident about the grades?' (Examination board staff)

Fit for purpose

Whether or not A-levels are fit for purpose was discussed in the focus groups, with the exception of the teacher focus groups. Participants expressed general concerns over reports that universities are questioning the utility of A-levels to prepare and select students for university places:

> I find it worrying that the universities are starting to question A-levels ... I don't know enough at the moment about that but I, that I do find worrying, given that we feed a lot of people into universities. (Examination board staff)

> In terms of the universities, they ... if they can't actually pick from the A-levels, you know the top students then it's not working for them. Aren't they really important as a stakeholder ... that the A-level system has to meet their basic requirements? (General public)

Some of these concerns were borne out in comments made by the admissions tutors:

> I think I trust it [the A-level system] up to a point but I'm not sure it's discriminating enough that's all. I trust that if you get a student with a good grade it presumably means that they're a good student potentially and able to cope with a higher education course but I think probably there needs to be some more discrimination at the top level … I mean when you're actually trying to look for the really good students and not just the good students. (Mathematics admissions tutor)

Some admissions tutors also commented that A-level results provide relatively imprecise information about students' abilities in a particular subject area and that they are perhaps too narrow in scope; expressing a preference for qualifications such as the International Baccalaureate. Having said this, they seemed to have a general trust in the processes used by examination boards to mark and publish A-level results. This raised an interesting distinction between trust in the 'nuts and bolts' of the A-level examination system, and trust in the qualification to provide learners with the skills and knowledge necessary to study at university level.

For students, whether or not A-level qualifications were fit for purpose took on a slightly different meaning. They were concerned that A-levels may not necessarily be relevant to or benefit them in their future careers:

> It needs to be clear what will get you where. I think that's really important, it's like somebody who wants to go and work in the music business does a music qualification, you're not going to get into music, it might help but really it's not the way … and it's like theatre studies, performing arts, if anyone did it, I'll hold my hands up, I did drama right and what they tell people and what the examining board… . 'Oh yeah you do this you'll become an actor'. Right, if that's true I should be like on Palm Springs beach sunning myself, getting a tan because I did drama… . (Student)

Mode of assessment

The methods used to assess candidates at A-level were a popular talking point in the focus groups. The general public, in particular, focused upon the fairness of coursework as a mode of assessment. Whilst some participants believed that course-work rightly provides those students who struggle with written examinations the opportunity to excel, others felt that coursework was open to abuse by students, teachers and parents. The comments below illustrate these opposing viewpoints:

> It makes it a lot easier or potentially a lot less stressful and a lot easier for the students to get all their grades if they can have 50 per cent on the exam and 50 per cent on the coursework. It would make it more accessible to people who learn differently and handle assessment differently. (General public)

> The thing that I'm not sure about is, on the coursework side now of the A-level system, I'm not sure whether it's the teacher that teaches that class that marks the coursework … and if it is then I think there's a real chance of kind of favouritism and in terms of that as well of parents who are a bit naughty. (General public)

In contrast, some admissions tutors, examination board staff, and teachers commented on the modularity of the A-level system. They felt that enabling students to re-sit modular exams several times may make it easier for students to achieve the higher grades, inflate pass rates, and unfairly advantage students taking modular examinations over students who sat linear examinations in the past. The following comments illustrate these points:

> Certainly from our point of view, in science subjects, the ability for students to take and re-take modules over and over has certainly made a difference in terms of grade shift because they're almost invariably able to improve their grades and that I think has been a major factor in terms of grade shift. Whether thats given us students who are any better I'm not sure ... that's not our perception. (Dentistry, admissions tutor)

> I think the modular system has made it easier to get higher grades because a lot of A-level pupils re-sit their modules, my own son did that, to, to up his marks. It's easier to re-sit a module than sort of the full exam. (Examination board staff)

In addition, admissions tutors expressed the opinion that the modular nature of the A-level system may discourage integrated learning. They felt that students tend to compartmentalise knowledge and information, rather than viewing the whole:

> I think the modular structure of A-level has its disadvantages because students see little things in little packets and don't see the connections ... so it's interesting year on year that you see the same topics that students have practically forgotten about, but they, they obviously knew them at some point, because they passed their modules. (Mathematics admissions tutor)

Discussion

This study represents the first step into trust research in the context of examinations. Research from the medical profession has shown trust to be a multi-dimensional concept (Hall *et al.*, 2001). The findings from the study support this contention. Participants discussed matters related to six broad aspects of the A-level examination system that appeared to impact upon their level of trust: 1) examination standards; 2) marking; 3) the syllabus; 4) communication and provision of information; 5) fitness of purpose and 6) mode of assessment. Much of the dialogue concerning these themes appeared to be negative, and reflects the media and political narrative in which A-levels are embedded.

Examination standards encompassed the maintenance of standards over time, as well as comparability of inter-board standards and inter-subject standards. Participants' discussions of marking largely centred around instances where marking had been found to be erroneous. Importantly, the participants demonstrated some misconceptions of marking procedures. There were concerns that the introduction of new marking technologies may introduce further inconsistency into the system when in practice these systems are designed to improve monitoring of examiners and reliability (Johnson *et al.*, 2010). Likewise, participants were concerned by re-marks, when the proportion of A-level re-marks that result in grade changes was less than half a percent of all A-level examination entries in 2011 (Ofqual, 2011). Such misconceptions suggest that trust in examinations is often based on perception, rather than fact. They also highlight the distinction between trust and trustworthiness

(Hardin, 2002)—the public's trust in examinations may waver, but this is not to say that the system is not entirely trustworthy. Finally, participants not only discussed trust in relation to marking in general, but also in relation to the marking of individual examiners. This distinction highlights the symbiotic relationship that exists between trust in organisations or systems and trust in individuals (Parker & Parker, 1993).

Trust in relation to the syllabus covered a number of aspects, depending upon the relationship of the qualification user to A-levels. Students discussed the syllabus in relation to question papers designed to test the syllabus. The fact that students appeared to be distrustful of examination questions, believing that they are in some way intended to trick or deceive them, is worrisome given that examinations are already known to be stressful, and anxiety-inducing events for students (Putwain, 2008 2009). Admissions tutors touched upon the content of the syllabus, whilst teachers focused upon the guidance and support they received in teaching syllabuses. For teachers, the provision of effective training, high-quality support materials, and being consulted during the development of new syllabuses were most likely to improve their confidence and trust in the syllabus, and subsequently in A-levels more generally.

Participants indicated that improved communication and provision of information would help to foster trust in A-levels. In accordance with findings from previous studies (Ipsos MORI, 2009) participants expressed confusion over the different examination boards and regulators that existed, and the functions they performed. Participants also expressed a desire for further information about examination board processes and the wider availability of results data. Whilst the idea of complete transparency is a controversial issue amongst educationalists (Newton, 2005), the findings from the study offer support for the arguments of O'Neill (2005), who advocates the *intelligible* communication of assessment information in order to allow the public to make informed trust judgements. Indeed, greater transparency about marking procedures may well have prevented the misconceptions displayed by participants in this study. For teachers, communication also included interactions with representatives of the examination system, again highlighting the fact that dealings with individuals can impact upon trust at the level of the system and vice versa.

Some participants questioned the fitness for purpose of A-levels, in terms of whether they prepared young people for university courses and later employment. This finding may be indicative of an erosion of trust; if qualifications are not perceived to be functioning correctly then the information they provide may not be valued by society. Having said this, the notion that A-levels should be fit for purpose does raise the question 'fit for whose purpose?' Had other stakeholder groups, such as employers, been included in the focus groups it seems likely that they would have had further expectations of A-levels. Is it realistically possible for A-levels to satisfy the requirements of a myriad of users? Or is it more likely that tensions will always exist due to the multiplicity of expectations and purposes for the qualification? Higton *et al.* (2012) conducted interviews and discussion groups with Higher Education representatives, teachers and employers on the fitness for purpose of A-levels. They concluded that although the potential purposes are numerous, they might not always conflict and the primary purpose of developing the necessary skills for Higher Education could subsume the others. However, even preparation for Higher Education is not straightforward. Some subjects are facilitative, in that students might not necessarily go on to study them further, but they act as general preparation for future study. What sociology and mathematics departments want from A-level Economics might well differ, for example. Thus, the implications of multiple expectations are that trust might be undermined even when it appears that a single purpose is prioritised.

In terms of mode of assessment, participants identified both coursework and modular schemes of assessment as potential factors that undermine their trust in A-levels. Both modes of assessment were thought to lower educational standards. With regard to modularity at A-level, there is evidence to suggest that the public's concerns may be justified. Hayward and McNicholl (2007), for example, investigated the costs and benefits of the increased use of a modular assessment scheme. They suggested that the proposed advantages of modularity—short-term goals and regular feedback, flexibility in curriculum design, improved progression possibilities—were outweighed by the disadvantages—such as fragmentation of knowledge and more instrumental approaches to assessment and learning. Poon Scott (2012), in her examination of resit policy at A-level, went further by arguing that allowing unlimited resits has resulted in grade inflation and that the learning styles encouraged by A-levels may render them unfit for purpose. Importantly, between June and September 2012 Ofqual conducted a consultation into A-level reform. Among other changes, the consultation showed support for both a reduction in internal assessment and the number of re-sit opportunities (Ofqual, 2012; Smith et al., 2012). Although many of the concerns raised in response to the consultation were in keeping with the findings of this research, how changes made to A-levels following the consultation will impact upon trust remains to be investigated.

It is important to note that the six dimensions of trust emerged from the data in their entirety. However, different groups' perceptions of trust differed substantially. Admissions tutors, for example, prioritised fitness for purpose. The different needs of the users of A-levels makes it difficult to engender the trust of all of its users all of the time.

Limitations of the study

Non-probability samples are usually considered satisfactory for exploratory research. However, it is possible that the strategies used to recruit participants for the study may have introduced a *volunteer bias*. Indeed, some of the teachers appeared to have particularly negative experiences of the A-level examination system, with re-marks for instance, and used the focus groups to vent their dissatisfaction. Consequently, the findings may suggest a lower level of trust in A-levels than is true of the wider population.

Another potential limitation concerns the key stakeholders omitted from the study. Examiners, parents and employers, for example, may well have different perceptions of trust in the A-level examination system. Having said this, a number of the teachers reported becoming examiners to improve command of their subject. Likewise, some of the members of the general public drew upon their experiences as parents when discussing trust in the A-level examination system. Thus, it is hoped that the conception of trust reported here is as complete as possible. Both the representativeness and validity of our conception of trust will be tested in subsequent quantitative research.

Finally, since definitions of trust are context dependent our conception of trust may not be transferable to other qualifications and countries. Again, this is something that needs to be explored in subsequent research.

Conclusions

Trust in examinations is likely to be multi-dimensional and may well be specific to given examinations and systems, due to the educationally and culturally specific role that examinations have in different societies. Trust in, for example, international test results such as PISA might well have different features than trust in A-levels.

Large-scale, high-stakes public examinations have to fulfil many purposes. Newton (2007) argued for a focus upon a single purpose for each test or examination. Such an approach might make the understanding and even fostering of trust in examinations more straightforward. However, Baird (2007) argued that public examinations are useful to society insomuch as they address several purposes and that different examinations or tests addressing each purpose would not fulfil the role that educational assessment has taken on. Indeed, expectations for the use of examination results are often invented after the examinations have been designed and even after they have been running for many years. For example, new expectations can arise about the extent to which one examination should be comparable with others. Within a context of multiple and changing expectations, getting a grip on the concept of trust in examinations is slippery. Our working model, based upon the research described here, involves six associated themes: 1) examination standards; 2) marking; 3) the syllabus; 4) communication and provision of information; 5) fitness of purpose and 6) mode of assessment. The extent to which these themes are dependent upon changing and innovative expectations that can be placed upon examinations remains an empirical question.

Acknowledgements

This work was supported initially by the Assessment and Qualifications Alliance and subsequently by the Economic and Social Research Council (grant number B91076D).

References

Anderson, L. A. & Dedrick, R.F. (1990). Development of the Trust in Physician scale: a measure to assess interpersonal trust in patient-physician relationships. *Psychological Reports*, 67, 1091–1100.

Baird, J. (2007). Alternative conceptions of comparability, in: P. Newton, J. Baird, H. Goldstein, H. Patrick & P. Tymms (Eds) *Techniques for monitoring the comparability of examination standards* (London, Qualifications and Curriculum Authority).

Baird, J. (2009). Country case study: England. Chapter 2, in: B. Vlaardingerbroek & N. Taylor (Eds) *External examination systems. Reliability, robustness and resilience.* New York, Cambria Press.

Barbour, R. S. (2001). Checklists for improving rigour in qualitative research: a case of the tail wagging the dog? *British Medical Journal*, 322 (7294), 1115–1117.

BBC (2012, 6 November). Available online at: http://www.bbc.co.uk/news/education-20223533

Calnan, M.W. & Sanford, E. (2004). Public trust in health care: The system or the doctor? *Quality and Safety in Health Care*, 13, 92–97.

Chamberlain, S. (2010). *Public perceptions of reliability.* Coventry, Office of Qualifications and Examinations Regulation. Available online at: http://www2.ofqual.gov.uk/files/Ofqual_10_4708_public_perceptions_reliability_report_08_03_10.pdf

Finch, H. & Lewis, J. (2003). Focus groups, in: J. Richie & J. Lewis (Eds) *Qualitative research practice: a guide for social science students and researchers* (London, Sage).

Goudge, J. & Gilson, L. (2005). How can trust be investigated? Drawing lessons from past experience. *Social Science & Medicine*, 61, 1439–1451.

Hall, M.A., Dugan, E., Zheng, B. & Mishra, A.K. (2001). Trust in physicians and medical institutions: what is it, can it be measured, and does it matter? *The Milbank Quarterly*, 79 (4), 613–639.

Hardin, R. (2002). *Trust and trustworthiness* (New York, Russell Sage Foundation).

Hayward, G. & McNicholl, J. (2007). Modular mayhem? A case study of the development of the A-level Science curriculum in England. *Assessment in Education:* Principles, Policy & Practice, 14(3), 335–351.

He, Q., Opposs, D. & Boyle, A. (2010). *A quantitative investigation into public perceptions of reliability in examination results in England.* Coventry, Office of Qualifications and Examinations Regulation. Available online at: http://www.ofqual.gov.uk/index.php?option=com_content & view=article & id=780.

Higton, J., Noble, J., Pope, S., Boal, N., Ginnis, S., Donaldson, R. & Greevy, H. (2012). Fit for purpose? The view of the higher education sector, teachers and employers of the suitability of A levels. Ofqual/12/5145.

Ipsos MORI (2003a). *Public confidence in the A level examination system.* Research study conducted for Qualifications and Curriculum Authority, March 2003.

Ipsos MORI. (2003b). *Confidence in the A level examination system: Autumn 2003.* Research study conducted for The Qualifications and Curriculum Authority.

Ipsos MORI. (2004). *Confidence in the A level examination system: Autumn 2004.* Research study conducted for The Qualifications and Curriculum Authority.

Ipsos MORI (2006a). *GCSEs and A levels: The experiences of teachers, students, parents and the general public.* Research study conducted for The Qualifications and Curriculum Authority, February 2006.

Ipsos MORI (2006b). *GCSEs and A levels: The experiences of teachers, students, parents and the general public.* Research study conducted for The Qualifications and Curriculum Authority, November 2006.

Ipsos MORI (2007). *GCSEs and A levels: The experiences of teachers, students, parents and the general public.* Research study conducted for The Qualifications and Curriculum Authority.

Ipsos MORI (2009). *Public perceptions of reliability in examinations.* A research study conducted for Ofqual.

Ipsos MORI (2010). *Perceptions of A levels and GCSEs—Wave 8.* Research study conducted for Ofqual.

Ipsos MORI (2011). *Perceptions of A levels and GCSEs—Wave 9.* Research study conducted for Ofqual.

Ipsos MORI (2012). *Perceptions of A levels, GCSEs and other qualifications—Wave 10.* Research study conducted on behalf of Ofqual.

Johnson, M., Nádas, R. & Bell, J.F. (2010). Marking essays on screen: an investigation into the reliability of marking extended subjective texts. *British Journal of Educational Technology*, 41 (5), 814–826.

Krueger, R.A. & Casey, M.A. (2000). *Focus groups, A practical guide for applied research* (London, Sage).

Murphy, R. (2004). *Grades of uncertainty: reviewing the use and misuses of examination results.* A report commissioned by the Association of Teachers and Lecturers.

Newton, P.E. (2005). The public understanding of measurement inaccuracy, *British Educational Research Journal*, 31(4), 419–442.

Newton, P.E. (2007). Clarifying the purpose of educational assessment, *Assessment in Education: Principles, Policy & Practice*, 14(2), 149–170.

Nisbet, I. (2007). *Intelligent regulation: trust and risk.* Available online at: http://webarchive. nationalarchives.gov.uk/+/http://www.ofqual.gov.uk/252.aspx (accessed 1 July 2012).

Ofqual (2011). *Ofqual publishes statistical bulletin into the Enquiries About Results (EAR) service.* Available online at: http://www2.ofqual.gov.uk/news-and-announcements/130/811 (accessed 21 November 2012).

Ofqual (2012). *Ofqual announces changes to A levels, 9 November.* Available online at: http://www. ofqual.gov.uk/news/ofqual-announces-changes-to-a-levels/ (accessed 19 November 2012).

O'Neill, O. (2005). *Assessment, public accountability and trust.* Available online at: http://www. cambridgeassessment.org.uk (accessed 25 May 2007).

Parker, A. & Tritter, J. (2006). Focus group method and methodology: current practice and recent debate. *International Journal of Research and Method in Education*, 29(1), 23–37.

Parker, S.L. & Parker, G.R. (1993). Why do we trust our congressman? *The Journal of Politics*, 55(2), 442–453.

Poon Scott, E. (2012). Short-term gain at long-term cost? How resit policy can affect student learning. *Assessment in Education: Principles, Policy and Practice*, 19(4), 431–449.

Putwain, D. W. (2008). Deconstructing test anxiety, *Emotional and Behavioural Difficulties*, 13 (2), 141–155.

Putwain, D. W. (2009). Assessment and examination stress in Key Stage 4, *British Educational Research Journal*, 35(3), 391–411.

Smith, J., Mitchell, T. & Grant, A. (2012). *Analysis of the consultation carried out into higher education involevement in GCE A levels and amended GCE A level criteria (design rules)*. Report commissioned by the Office of Qualifications and Examinations Regulation. Available online at: http://www.ofqual.gov.uk/files/2012-11-07-Analysis-of-the-consultation-into-he-involvement-in-a-levels-and-amended-criteria.pdf (accessed 19 November 2012).

Spencer, L., Ritchie, J. & O'Connor, W. (2003). Analysis: practices, principles and processes, in: J. Ritchie & J. Lewis (Eds) *Qualitative research: a guide for social science students and researchers.* London, Sage.

Straten, G.F.M., Friele, R.D. & Groenewegen, P.P. (2002). Public trust in Dutch health care. *Social Science and Medicine*, 55, 227–234.

Sztompka, P. (1999). *Trust: a sociological theory.* New York, Cambridge University Press.

Tate, N. (2005). Maintaining trust in public assessment systems: an international perspective. Paper presented at the *Cambridge Assessment Conference*, 17 October. Available online at: www.cambridgeassessment.org.uk (accessed 25 May 2007).

Warmington, P. & Murphy, R. (2004). Could do better? Media depictions of UK educational assessment results. *Journal of Education Policy*, 19(3), 285–299.

Watt, H., Newell, C., Winnett, R. & Paton, G. (2011a). Cheating the system: how examiners tip off teachers. *Daily Telegraph*, 8 December, 1.

Watt, H., Newell, C., Winnett, R. & Paton, G. (2011b). 'There's so little content we don't know how we got it through'. *Daily Telegraph*, 9 December, 1.

Wiliam, D. (1996). Standards in examinations: a matter of trust? *The Curriculum Journal*, 7(3), 293–306.

Towards improving public understanding of judgement practice in standards-referenced assessment: an Australian perspective

Val Klenowski
Queensland University of Technology, Australia

Curriculum and standards-referenced assessment reform in accountability contexts are increasingly dominated by the use of testing, evidence, comparative analyses of achievement data and policy as numbers all of which have given rise to a set of related developments. Internationally these developments towards the use of standards for assessment and accountability purposes have placed new demands on teachers, their students and parents. How measures of quality are communicated in policy, when represented as standards, how they are promulgated and how they are used in practice, by whom and for what purposes become central questions to an understanding of current assessment practice. The argument developed focuses on the importance of improving public understanding of the implications of standards-driven reforms for teachers in making judgements about the quality of student work. Research of teachers' use of standards, judgement and moderation for both accountability and improvement of learning purposes are drawn upon in arguing the case for increased public understanding of the teacher's role in classroom assessment and pedagogy. Quality processes that aim to develop and to sustain the dependability of teacher judgement within summative assessment systems, and that build trust in teacher judgement practice by the teachers themselves, the parents, the students and the public in particular contexts, are analysed. The role of judgement in assessment, who controls this field and whose judgement counts are critically considered.

Introduction

Internationally there has been a move towards standards-referenced assessment with countries such as Australia developing a National Curriculum and

Achievement Standards, New Zealand adopting National Standards for literacy and numeracy that involve schools making and reporting judgements about the reading, writing and mathematics achievement of children up to Year 8 (the end of primary school) and in Canada, classroom assessment standards aimed at the improvement of assessment practice of K-12 education are being formulated. Standards-driven reform has major implications for teachers' work. The consequences of adopting a standards-driven approach to educational change by systems are often under-estimated with the unintended effects not fully understood by either the policy writers or the public, including parents. It is for these reasons that the contention developed in this article relates to the teacher's role, which, it is argued, remains central to policy focused on the improvement of the quality of education and educational standards.

Today governments are hungry for information and are propelled to implement such reforms because of the perceived declining scores as reported in international comparative analyses of achievement data of tests such as PISA and TIMSS. Governments have readily responded to the PISA shock with centralised curriculum development, with increased testing and with loss of faith in teachers' judgements. The media too has seized on 'numbers' and declining scores from international tables to present a view of education that is distorted or in a state of crisis. The belief that tests and examinations are the only objective and reliable representations of student achievement become accepted by the public. Ironically, when standards-driven reforms are initiated teacher judgement remains fundamental, yet research conducted in this current context is limited. The research that has been conducted in relation to teacher judgement has focused more on inter-rater reliability in relation to the training of examiners (Johnson et al., 2001; Baird et al., 2004; Greatorex, 2008). The importance of raising awareness and informing the public of the significance of teacher judgement in the use of standards for valid and reliable assessment practice is presented.

The quality processes that help to develop and sustain the dependability of teacher judgement within summative assessment systems are those that have, and build, trust in teacher judgement practice by the teachers themselves, the parents, the students and the public. Recent empirical research conducted in Queensland, Australia (Klenowski & Adie, 2009; Klenowski & Wyatt-Smith, 2010; Adie et al., 2011; Connolly et al., 2011) is used to explicate the role of judgement in assessment and to analyse critically who controls this field and whose judgement counts. It is emphasised at the outset that, unlike places such as England and the USA, Queensland has a history of externally moderated school-based assessment in the senior years (Years 11 and 12) with standards-based and teacher-moderated assessment at the core of the Queensland senior assessment model. However, the introduction of the use of standards by teachers of Years 1–10 was a new experience for many.

Identifying the issues

It is important to improve the understanding of those outside the specialist assessment community including parents, teachers, students and the wider public, and policy influencers such as media and non-teaching education professionals, of the implications of standards-driven reforms on teachers' judgement practice. Research in the field of teacher judgement to examine how standards-referenced assessment practice connects with curriculum and learning and to identify the various purposes of assessment in contexts of accountability, with increased expectations of improved standards, becomes a priority. Understanding the implications of standards-driven reforms for teachers' pedagogic practice as they work to improve the standards of the quality of student work on the one hand, and attend to equity issues on the other, is also in need of critical attention and understanding by those in the profession but also the public.

Reconsidering the purposes of assessment

To begin, clarity concerning the understanding of the purposes of assessment is vital. Reference is made to the work of Paul Newton (2007, 2010) who has recently reconsidered the purpose of assessment from a categorisation of three levels. The judgement level is the first of these. This level of purpose relates to the technical aim of an assessment event, which includes standards-referenced judgements expressed as grades or marks. The second level of assessment purpose is the decision level, which concerns the use of an assessment judgement for enacting a decision, action or process. Third is the impact level, which relates to the intended impacts of an assessment system, such as in ensuring that students are motivated to learn and that all students learn the intended curriculum for each subject. These are impacts specifically attributable to the design of the particular assessment system not to the characteristics of the wider education system within which it operates (Newton, 2007, p. 150). This reconsideration of the purposes of assessment will be used to illustrate how the first of these levels becomes prominent in the move to standards-referenced assessment systems.

In countries such as Australia and New Zealand, where standards-referenced systems have been introduced there has been limited opportunity and consequently a paucity of research to inform policy developments. These reforms have occurred quickly for as Patricia Broadfoot and Paul Black (2004, p. 9) noted, 'decisions about assessment procedures—particularly those concerning high stakes testing of various kinds—are as often based on perceived *political* appeal as they are on a systematic knowledge on the scientific evidence concerning fitness for purpose'. This assertion very much applies to the Australian context and as argued elsewhere if national testing programmes are to genuinely improve outcomes, as distinct from reporting them, then we *need to acknowledge that it is the teacher not the test that is the primary agent of change* (Klenowski, 2012a). The preoccupation in the media with results and the comparative analyses of schools' performances deprives public understanding of the contextual conditions and sociocultural influences that impact on students' learning and achievement.

The judgement level of purpose has come to dominate teachers' work in Australia and New Zealand because standards require teachers to generate a particular kind of judgement outcome, such as a grade linked to an achievement standard as in Australia, or National Standards as in New Zealand. In Australia, teachers are expected to use their standards-referenced judgements to report twice yearly on students' achievement expressed as a grade from A to E. At the decision level of purpose it is the use of the assessment results that become significant when, for instance, a student seeks entry to a particular university course of study. The social or educational impact of assessment is illustrated when learners are motivated to improve the quality of their learning or when teachers align their teaching with the requirements of the Australian curriculum. In each of these levels of purpose, the teacher's role remains central, and teacher judgement becomes fundamental. Yet, teacher judgement research in this context remains limited and findings are in their infancy in these countries experiencing recent standards-driven reform.

Historically there has been an emphasis on the distinction between formative and summative, although Newton (2007, p. 155) questions whether there is actually a meaningful distinction to be drawn at all. Summative, he argues, is characterised as a type of assessment judgement in that it operates at the judgement level of discourse, while formative characterises a type of use to which assessment judgements are put and therefore operates at the decision level of discourse. At both these levels the teacher's role is heightened in relation to use of assessment data or feedback to make judgements or decisions using standards. The distinction referred to by Newton will be used to illustrate how summative assessment or the judgement level has increasingly encroached on teacher's teaching and classroom practice.

The teacher–student dynamic

John Hattie has recently emphasised the quality of teaching (which is taken to include the teacher's assessment practices), and teacher contributions to student learning (2009, 2012). In Hattie's synthesis (2009, p. 35) of many meta-analyses he concluded that '[i]t is what teachers get the students to do in the class that emerged as the strongest component of the accomplished teacher's repertoire, rather than what the teacher specifically, does.' It is when teachers make use of assessment data to inform their students of what actions or decisions they need to take to improve their learning, and when they use that data to motivate their students to take action, that matters. It is also when teachers, themselves, use the assessment data to make decisions and take actions in relation to their own teaching, that the decision level of purpose of assessment becomes most explicit. This decision level of purpose of assessment has most relevance for the principal stakeholders in this exchange——the students. They are the recipients of the outcomes of these levels of purpose of assessment and there is no denying that, 'assessment shapes who and what we are and cannot be treated as a neutral measure of abilities and skills that are independent of society' (Nietzsche cited by Stobart, 2008, p. 6). The significance of the judgement level of purpose of assessment is again emphasised.

Hattie too argues that we should not overlook those who are best positioned to evaluate the teachers—the students who share the classroom with the teacher day in and day out. He claims that: 'what matters are conceptions of teaching, learning, assessment, and teachers having expectations that *all* students can progress, that achievement for *all* is changeable (and not fixed), and that progress for *all* is understood and articulated. It is teachers who are open to experience, learn from errors, seek and learn from feedback from students, who foster effort, clarity, and engagement in learning' (Hattie, 2009, p. 35). The decision level of assessment is highlighted here and the way that assessment is integral to the teaching and learning cycle is explicated.

Research conducted in Australia illustrates how the teacher–student dynamic operates at the different levels of purpose of assessment in the context of standards-driven reform (Klenowski & Adie, 2009; Wyatt-Smith *et al.*, 2010). With the increase in summative assessment, or the judgement level of purpose, teachers' effective use of standards to assess the quality of student learning is important, for it is this level of purpose that has far-reaching effects on students' learning and life trajectories.

Australian context

In Australia the judgement-level purpose has become prominent with the introduction of the National Assessment Programme—Literacy and Numeracy (NAPLAN) in 2008 and the development and uptake in 2012 by most jurisdictions of a national curriculum and achievement standards. At the time of the launch of the federal government's *MySchool* website (www.myschool.com) it was claimed that NAPLAN was designed to serve the national interest by measuring student outcomes in literacy and numeracy. Today each individual school's performance is published on the *MySchool* website which the federal government maintains achieves transparency for parents to evaluate schools' performance, and to target schools that are underperforming. Each school's profile page includes a colour coded summary table of the school's NAPLAN results to identify substantial differences between the results from the school compared with the Australian average and the results of statistically similar schools (ACARA, 2009).

Comparisons between the states now tend to dominate media reports with the rather unsurprising outcome of issues of low equity reported each year. In addition, the lack of alignment with curriculum and assessment practice has had the predictable corrupting effects of high-stakes accountability testing on learning and teaching (Gardner, 2006; Harlen, 2006; Nichols & Berliner, 2008; Klenowski & Wyatt-Smith, 2012; Klenowski, 2012b).

In Australia while the judgement level of purpose has come to prominence it could also be said that the impact level of purpose is evident in the way in which change to the assessment system has come about. Each jurisdiction within Australia is responsible for curriculum development, implementation, assessment and reporting. States and territories are working with the Australian Curriculum, Assessment and Reporting Authority (ACARA), an independent authority, towards a more nationally consistent approach. Yet each jurisdiction is developing its own plan for implementation and teacher support. The case of Queensland is analysed, and critically considered, since it is in this context that recent research concerning the implications of standards-driven reform for teacher judgement practice has been conducted.

The assessment types practised in Queensland include teacher assessment, at the judgement level for the award of A–E grades reported to students every semester in every year in every subject. School-based testing and assessment also comprises the NAPLAN tests which are conducted in May each year. Students receive their results in September, and the school receives diagnostic information in December or January. The results are reported on the *MySchool* website with attention increasingly given to the results for individual students. Teacher judgement remains central to all performance evidence, which includes that generated in standardised testing as well as in classroom-based programmes.

Achievement standards

Teachers' assessment practices have been challenged and jurisdictions have had to consider the level of support they provide to teachers in these times of assessment change. ACARA has had the responsibility for the development of a national curriculum of content descriptions and achievement standards. This is claimed to be ostensibly a futures-oriented curriculum that incorporates more open-ended questions, which require students to apply their understanding and to demonstrate their skills. The achievement standards are published features of quality against which teacher judgement can now be held accountable or scrutinised. They comprise a written descriptor plus annotated student work samples, to indicate an expectation of the quality of learning that students should typically demonstrate by a particular juncture in their schooling. An example of the Year 9 (14-year-old) achievement standard for Science follows.

> By the end of Year 9, students explain chemical processes and natural radioactivity in terms of atoms and energy transfers and describe examples of important chemical reactions. They describe models of energy transfer and apply these to explain phenomena. They explain global features and events in terms of geological processes and timescales. They analyse how biological systems function and respond to external changes with reference to interdependencies, energy transfers and flows of matter. They describe social and technological factors that have influenced scientific developments and predict how future applications of science and technology may affect people's lives.

Students design questions that can be investigated using a range of inquiry skills. They design methods that include the control and accurate measurement of variables and systematic collection of data and describe how they considered ethics and safety. They analyse trends in data, identify relationships between variables and reveal inconsistencies in results. They analyse their methods and the quality of their data, and explain specific actions to improve the quality of their evidence. They evaluate others' methods and explanations from a scientific perspective and use appropriate language and representations when communicating their findings and ideas to specific audiences. (www.acara.edu.au/curriculum)

This standard is designed to indicate the achievement that students should typically demonstrate by the end of Year 9. At the impact level of assessment, teachers in Australia are required to assess students' application of their understandings and the development of their skills such as inquiry, analysis, investigation and reflection. Teachers are provided with student work samples, the related assessment task, the student's response and annotations identifying the qualities of learning evident in the student's response aligned to the achievement standard. ACARA's advice is that together the achievement standard plus the annotated work samples help teachers to make judgements about whether students have achieved the standard. An essential process remains missing from ACARA's guidance, which is *how the standards are to be used* at the different levels of purpose of assessment and what this means for teachers' practice, for the various levels of the assessment system from the jurisdictional level in terms of the additional support and resources that teachers will require to use the standards effectively, to the classroom level in terms of the implications for their practice.

The standards provide a common set of stated reference points and the way they are represented conveys expectations of quality and levels of performance. Teachers are now increasingly challenged at all levels of the system—student, classroom, school, community, district, regional, state and national—as they are being told on the one hand to increase the NAPLAN results of their students, and on the other to make standards-referenced judgements on the basis of the achievement standards and exemplar materials. From the research conducted in Queensland it is evident that teachers require a greater range of resource support and professional development. Education departments of the jurisdictions are providing resources and development opportunities; however, continued monitoring and evaluation will be required to establish the level of support required for the effective use of standards to achieve the intended goals of quality learning outcomes.

Implications for teachers' practice

Throughout Australia teachers will now be expected to use the achievement standards in their assessment practice. Standards-referenced reforms, plus the shift towards a futures-oriented curriculum, mean that teachers can no longer rely solely on assessment formats such as standardised, paper-and-pencil, multiple-choice or short-answer tests. These formats are considered reductionist in that students cannot demonstrate the extent of their knowledge fully. The level of sophistication of their skills and the depth of their understanding is often more accurately assessed through the application of these understandings and skills by demonstrations as in live performances or presentations. The implications are that teachers' planning, and assessment programmes of high quality, will have to be designed so that students are provided with the variety of opportunities to demonstrate their achievement of the curriculum content, and the development of their skills and understandings inherent in the achievement standards for the Australian Curriculum learning areas.

Given the variety of skills and understandings that will be assessed teachers will now be expected to assess folios of work, gathered over the reporting periods to the end of a semester or the end of the year, for an on-balance judgement of the standard achieved. The assessment of folios of work involves moderation practice as a necessary supportive process for teachers' judgement practice to address the threats to validity through 'construct-irrelevant variance' or 'construct under-representation' (Messick, 1989; Klenowski, 2002). These demands for quality assessment tasks and assessment of folios of work have significant implications for the levels of support and resources made available to teachers.

Queensland's approach

The framework, to support Queensland teachers in 2012 in the use of achievement standards builds on prior research (Klenowski & Wyatt-Smith, 2010; Connolly *et al.*, 2011) and policy developments (ACACA, 1995; QSA, 2012) and includes guidelines and advice, resource development and professional development, communicated using ICT infrastructure (http://www.qsa.qld.edu.au/10195.html). For the past six years the Queensland Studies Authority (QSA) has continued to develop the Queensland Comparable Assessment Tasks or QCATs, which teachers have used in Years 4, 6 and 9 in English, mathematics and science (http://www.qsa.qld.edu.au/3163.html). These tasks have been developed, refined and more recently re-designed to assist teachers to understand the qualities in student work indicative of the national achievement standards. They are derived from the concept of 'rich tasks' and are performance oriented (http://education.qld.gov.au/corporate/newbasics/html/richtasks/richtasks.html).

The QCATs, which now align with the national curriculum, are intended to model quality task design at the appropriate level of demand to demonstrate understanding as well as skills of critical thinking, reflection and investigation. Designing tasks to provide students with relevant opportunities to demonstrate disciplinary knowledge at a particular standard and also to apply that knowledge to be assessed by presentation or performance requires a more sophisticated approach to assessment task design. As seen from the example of the standard for Year 9 science students, they are now expected to demonstrate skills in inquiry, analysis and design as well as content knowledge. The Queensland Studies Authority at a systems level has invested in support for teachers by developing QCATs to model exemplary assessment tasks pitched at the appropriate standard to fulfill the demands of the achievement standards. Further, to meet the diverse needs of students, different assessment formats have been designed. Again these formats incorporate more open-ended questions requiring students to apply their understanding and to demonstrate their skills, heightening the importance of teacher judgement (www.qsa.qld.edu.au).

Moderation

Moderation or 'social moderation' (Linn, 1993) is a process involving practitioners in discussion and debate about their interpretations of the quality of assessed work. Moderation is a social practice that involves teachers exchanging views about the standard or grade awarded to a representative sample of teacher-assessed student work. A central purpose is to promote and support consistency, comparability and inter-rater reliability in teacher judgement (Maxwell, 2009; Klenowski & Wyatt-Smith, in press). This practice is considered appropriate particularly with the introduction of a standards-referenced system, and is an important way in which standards are promulgated. Teachers explicate their interpretations of assessment criteria and standards with the aim of reaching agreement regarding the standard assigned to the student work or portfolio of evidence being scrutinised. Social moderation is thereby based on teacher professional judgement as opposed to statistical approaches of equating.

'Consensus moderation' is a term that has been used to describe this form of social moderation. While consensus is often emphasised in definitions of moderation, during the meeting different interpretations of the standards will emerge as practitioners explain their judgement practice or when they state their interpretations publicly. It is from such instances of disagreement, however, that new knowledge or understanding can be generated in relation to the interpretation of the standards. This interpretivist perspective aligns with a sociocultural view of learning and assessment (Gipps, 1999; Scarino, 2005; Murphy & Hall, 2008; Pryor & Crossouard, 2008) in that moderation as a social practice acknowledges that the cultural context, the texts, the teachers' beliefs and values will mediate their judgements. Moderation meetings provide the opportunity for the development of professional learning communities where the enhancement of the teachers' learning about standards and judgement practices becomes possible. The development of a professional community of practice or an assessment community, either within the school or between schools, has been identified as a way of increasing confidence in teachers' judgement by the teachers themselves and among the users of the assessments (Harlen, 2005).

Using standards for the first time is challenging for teachers as their confidence in how to use the standards develops over time. It is through the application of the standards in the assessment of student work that the standards acquire meaning for the teachers and they gain improved understanding of the features of quality for the particular standard. This is because standards when written as verbal descriptors require interpretation and application in a community of practice. The dependability of teachers' judgements is sustained through moderation (Harlen, 2005) and it is in the conversations that teachers have in this process that their understanding of the learning goals and related criteria are developed. Standards need to be validated through interpretation and negotiation in moderation practice and should be empirically derived.

As identified by Royce Sadler (1998) when teachers are engaged in making a judgement of student work they draw on a variety of intellectual and experiential resources. Teachers require a superior knowledge about the subject content or the material that students need to learn. They also need an understanding of the criteria and standards (or performance expectations) that are appropriate to the assessment task. Furthermore, they require evaluative skills in making judgements about students' efforts on similar tasks. Finally a 'set of attitudes or dispositions towards teaching, as an activity, and towards learners, including their own ability to empathise with students who are learning, their desire to help students develop, improve and do better, their personal concern for the feedback and veracity of their own judgements, and their patterns in offering help' (Sadler, 1998, pp. 80–82) are further requirements.

Research

How standards inform and 'regulate' teacher judgement of student work in the middle years of schooling was the subject of a large-scale Australian Research Council Linkage project. The study was conducted in Queensland, with the support of the Queensland Studies Authority (QSA), to identify also how best to support teachers in times of standards-referenced assessment with increased demands on their practice. In this study teachers were using achievement standards for summative assessment or at the judgement level of assessment purpose for the first time.

The qualitative study was conducted over a period of three years with 49 schools and 89 teachers. A total of 164 interviews were conducted pre-moderation (90) and post-moderation (74), associated with observations of 75 moderation sessions. Data were organised into sets, Nvivo software was used to code and categorise data, emergent themes were progressively refined. A constant comparative method and an interpretivist approach were utilised to identify patterns in the data. Sociocultural theories of learning and assessment (Wenger, 1998; Murphy & Hall, 2008; Pryor & Crossouard, 2008; Rogoff, 2008) underpinned the analysis and provided the analytic lens to identify and explain the many influences on teachers' judgements beyond the criteria and standards linked to the assessment tasks.

Key research findings as they relate to the use of standards, moderation and teacher judgement support the contention that it is the teacher's judgement that counts. The findings also indicate the significant challenges that emerge for teachers to understand and interpret the standards when they are first introduced and then for teachers to develop an understanding of how the standards shape their assessment and teaching practices. A further challenge for teachers presents when they apply their skills in the use of the standards to enable the participation of the range of diverse learners in their classes. The implications for future policy and practice are identified following a discussion of the relevant key findings.

Discussion of key findings

A significant finding from the research was that the provision of standards and annotated samples of student work were found to be necessary but insufficient for teachers to develop consistency in their judgements of student work and comparability in their standards-referenced judgements (Wyatt-Smith *et al.*, 2010). Standards are historic in nature in that they are socially constructed at a particular point in time and can therefore be subject to change over time. Further support such as that provided in moderation meetings where teachers can develop and inform their judgement practice was found to be necessary. As teachers come together in moderation meetings and articulate their interpretations of the evidence in the student work in relation to the standards, they develop a level of confidence and understanding of how the standards are used. Standards, annotated samples with a commentary articulating the trade-offs made to arrive at that particular judgement, and moderation practice are all required. Providing teachers with exemplars that have associated commentaries helps to develop and support the development and improvement of teachers' judgement practice in standards-referenced assessment systems.

If teacher use of standards is to fulfill the assessment purposes at the level of judgement *and* the decision level of improved learning then greater clarity about these purposes and functions of standards would help illustrate and realise the significance of the teachers' role. In Australia the functions of achievement standards have been identified as clarifying the expected quality of learning to be achieved, providing a useful discourse with which teachers can discuss the student's current achievement level and progress to date, and implications for development with the students and their parents. It has also been reported that achievement standards help to identify those students whose rate of progress puts them at risk of being unable to reach satisfactory achievement levels in later years (National Curriculum Board, 2008). Given the growing global trend for using standards not just for accountability but also for the purpose of improving learning, clarity about how standards can and are to be used to achieve these purposes requires policy and research support.

The way standards are formulated influences not only their representation but also suggests a particular approach to judgement. Standards provide a common set of stated reference points; however, if they are represented in a matrix format it has been found that teachers are more likely to adopt an analytic approach to judgement (Klenowski & Wyatt-Smith, 2010). Using an analytic approach often results in the weighting of criteria and the process of judgement becomes atomised in that the assessor allocates marks to particular criteria with a summing up of the marks to award the grade. If, however, the standards are represented in the form of continua then a more holistic approach to judgement is taken (Sadler, 2007). This approach results in a more evaluative exercise and is often related to the nature of the assessment task, which requires a complex response in that there is no one correct answer. Given the increased cognitive demands of a futures-oriented curriculum and the more open-ended nature of the assessment tasks a more holistic approach to judgement would appear to be more suitable and a representation of standards as continua more appropriate. To ensure the validity and reliability of the interpretations of the standards when adopting a holistic approach will entail teachers engaging in moderation practice.

Understanding how the representation of standards influences the approach to judgement and the promulgation of standards becomes a further significant consideration. To achieve valid and reliable use of standards for learning improvement will therefore involve teacher judgement and moderation practice that includes the use of exemplars with the provision of a commentary to explain the trade-offs and configural properties of judgement (Cooksey *et al.*, 2007; Wyatt-Smith & Klenowski, 2012), the interpretation of evidence, consistency and comparability in judgements of common learning goals.

Conclusion

Teacher judgement is under-researched and in its infancy and while there is a substantial research base on inter-rater reliability (Baird *et al.*, 2004) much of this research has been conducted in the context of examinations not at the level of teacher judgement practice or at the decision level of purpose of assessment.

If the introduction of a standards-driven approach to reform is to achieve the intended goals of improvement towards excellence in learning and teaching then investment in the teacher workforce by authorities, government and universities (pre-service education) in support of a shift to a more balanced approach to assessment that recognises and supports teacher judgement practice is required. With standards-driven reform teacher judgement and moderation are both necessary. As outlined in this article:

- guidance in how to use the standards at the different levels of assessment purpose;
- the provision of annotated exemplars with commentaries that explain the trade offs and configural properties of the judgement process (Wyatt-Smith & Klenowski, 2012);
- the identification of evidence in the student work to support the teacher's judgement in the explication of interpretations of standards in communities of practice for consistency and comparability purposes; and
- moderation practice

are *all* needed in a standards-based system.

Teachers are viewed as the primary change agents, their judgement practices are integral to the requirements of assessment tasks and expectations of quality performance. They are best placed to identify important steps for students to improve in their learning and to develop useful insights about how best to change pedagogy to meet a student's particular learning needs. Judgement is at the very heart of assessment yet an appreciation of the importance of the quality of evidence, interpretation of the standard and moderation practice has largely been restricted to the academic community. It is time for policy officers, and those outside the specialist assessment community, particularly parents, when considering standards-driven policy reform to be more informed of the value and importance of the teacher's role in judgement practice and what this implies for policy and resource support to achieve the intended outcomes of improved learning and teaching through the effective use of standards.

'Where has all the judgement gone?' by Ralph B. Peck is a seminal article that derived from the Fifth Laurits Bjerrum Memorial Lecture which he delivered in Oslo, Norway in 1980. It is just as important for us as educators, for although Peck was an engineer he was also an educator. The significance of this article lies in the answer to this question that Peck raised:

> It [judgement] has gone where the rewards of professional recognition and advancement are greatest—to the design office where the sheer beauty of analysis is often separated from reality. It has gone to the research institutions, into the fascinating effort to idealize the properties of real materials for purpose of analysis and into the solution of intricate problems of stress distribution and deformation of idealized materials. The incentive to make a professional reputation leads the best people in these directions. (DiBiagio & Flaate, 2000, p. 61)

There are parallels here with education in that when we ask, 'whose judgement counts in a standards-referenced system?' the answer lies with teachers. Yet, as identified by Peck in the context of engineering, 'designers and regulatory bodies tend to place increasing reliance on analytical procedures of growing complexity and to discount judgement as a nonquantitive, undependable contributor to design' (DiBiagio, 2000, p. 59). In Australia we have also witnessed a discounting of teacher judgement and valid forms of teacher assessment as 'nonquantitive' and 'undependable' with the increased emphasis on NAPLAN results and testing data.

In education, trust in teacher judgement (O'Neill, 2002; Harlen, 2005) needs to be maintained. As educators there is room for development in our understanding of what teacher judgement entails and how it is used and enacted. Such research will not only help to develop improved teacher judgement but also ultimately lead to higher standards in learning for this and future generations of students to live healthy, productive, ethical and safe lives.

Acknowledgements

The author wishes to acknowledge that some ideas presented in this article derive from a Linkage Project funded by the Australian Research Council. The contributions from the Industry Partners, the Queensland Studies Authority (QSA), the National Council for Curriculum and Assessment of the Republic of Ireland, the author's fellow chief investigator Professor Claire Wyatt-Smith, and researchers Dr Lenore Adie and Peta Colbert, are also acknowledged and thanked.

References

Adie, L.E., Klenowski, V. & Wyatt-Smith, C. (2011). Towards an understanding of teacher judgement in the context of social moderation. *Educational Review*, 64(2), 223–240.

Australian, Curriculum, Assessment and Certification Authorities (1995). *Guidelines for assessment quality and equity*. Brisbane, Queensland Studies Authority.

Australian Curriculum, Assessment and Reporting Authority (2009). *Curriculum design paper*. Available online at: http://www.acara.edu.au/verve/_resources/Curriculum_Design_Paper_.pdf (accessed 16 June 2009).

Baird, J., Greatorex, J. & Bell, J.F. (2004). What makes marking reliable? Experiments with UK examinations. *Assessment in Education: Principles, Policy and Practice*, 11(3), 331–348.

Broadfoot, P. & Black, P. (2004). Refining assessment? The first ten years of assessment in education. *Assessment in Education: Principles, Policy and Practice*, 11(1), 7–27.

Connolly, S., Klenowski, V. & Wyatt-Smith, C. (2011). Moderation and consistency of teacher judgement: teachers' views. *British Educational Research Journal*, 38(4), 593–614.

Cooksey, R.W., Freebody, P. & Wyatt-Smith, C. (2007). Assessment as judgement-in-context: analysing how teachers evaluate students' writing. *Educational Research and Evaluation*, 13(5), 401–434.

DiBiagio, E. & Flaate, K. (Eds) (2000). *Ralph B. Peck engineer, educator, a man of judgement*. Oslo, Norwegian Geotechnical Institute.

Gardner, J. (2006). *Assessment and learning*. London, Sage.

Gipps, C. (1999). Socio-cultural aspects of assessment, in: P.D. Pearson & A. Iran Nejad (Eds) *Review of Research in Education, 24*. Washington, American Educational Research Association, 355–392.

Harlen, W. (2005). Trusting teachers' judgement: research evidence of the reliability and validity of teachers' assessment used for summative purposes. *Research Papers in Education*, 20(3), 245–270.

Harlen, W. (2006). On the relationship between assessment for formative and summative purposes, in: J. Gardner (Ed.) *Assessment and learning*. London, Sage, 103–117.

Hattie, J.A. (2009) *Visible learning: A synthesis of over 800 meta-analyses relating to achievement*. London, Routledge.

Johnson, R.L., Penny, J. & Gordon, B. (2001). Score resolution and the interrater reliability of holistic scores in rating essays. *Written Communication*, 18, 229–249.

Klenowski, V. (2002). *Developing portfolios for learning and assessment: processes and principles.* London, RoutledgeFalmer.

Klenowski, V. (2012a). Sustaining teacher professionalism in the context of standards referenced assessment reform, in: A. Luke, A. Woods & K. Weir (Eds) *Curriculum syllabus design and equity: a primer and model.* London, Routledge, 88–102.

Klenowski, V. (2012b). Raising the stakes the challenges for teacher assessment. *Australian Educational Researcher*, 39(2), 173–192.

Klenowski, V. & Adie, L.E. (2009). Moderation as judgement practice. reconciling system level accountability and local level practice. *Curriculum Perspectives*, 29(1), 10–28.

Klenowski, V. & Wyatt-Smith, C.M. (2010). Standards, teacher judgement and moderation in the contexts of national curriculum and assessment reform. *Assessment Matters*, 2, 107–131.

Klenowski, V. & Wyatt-Smith, C. (2012). The impact of high stakes testing: the Australian story. *Assessment in Education: Principles, Policy and Practice*, 19(1), 65–79.

Klenowski, V. & Wyatt-Smith, C. (in press). *Assessment for education: a guide for students, teachers and researchers.* London, Sage.

Linn, R.L. (1993). Linking results of distinct assessments. *Applied Measurement in Education*, 6 (1), 83–102.

Linn, R. (2003). Accountability: responsibility and reasonable expectations. *Educational Researcher*, 3(7), 3–13.

Maxwell, G.S. (2009). Defining standards for the 21st century, in: C.M. Wyatt-Smith & J.J. Cumming (Eds) *Educational assessment in the 21st century.* Dordrecht, Springer, 263–286.

Messick, S. (1989). Validity, in: R.L. Linn (Ed.) *Educational measurement.* New York, Macmillan, 13–103.

Murphy, P. & Hall, K. (Eds) (2008). *Learning and practice. agency and identities.* London, Sage.

National Curriculum Board (2008). *The shape of the national curriculum: a proposal for discussion.* Available online at: http://www.ncb.org.au/our_work/preparing_for_2009.html (accessed 5 November 2008).

Newton, P.E. (2007). Clarifying the purposes of educational assessment. *Assessment in Education: Principle, Policy and Practice*, 14(2), 149–170.

Newton, P.E. (2010). The multiple purposes of assessment. *International Encyclopedia of Education*, 3, 392–396.

Nichols, S.L. & Berliner, D.C. (2008). *Collateral damage: how high stakes testing corrupts America's schools.* Cambridge, MA, Harvard Education Press.

O'Neill, O. (2002). *A question of trust: the BBC Reith Lectures.* Cambridge, Cambridge University Press.

Pryor, J. & Crossouard, B. (2008). A socio-cultural theorisation of formative assessment. *Oxford Review of Education*, 34(1), 1–20.

Queensland Studies Authority (2012) *Using the learning area standards descriptors, Advice on implementing the Australian curriculum P-10.* Available online at: www.qsa.qld.edu.au (accessed 23 March 2012).

Rogoff, B. (2008). Thinking with the tools and institutions of culture, in: P. Murphy & K. Hall (Eds) *Learning and practice. agency and identities.* London, Sage, 49–70.

Sadler, D.R. (1998). Formative assessment: revisiting the territory. *Assessment in Education: Principles, Policy & Practice*, 5(1), 77–84.

Sadler, R. (2007). Perils in the meticulous specification of goals and assessment criteria. *Assessment in Education: Principles, Policy & Practice*, 14(3), 387–392.

Scarino, A. (2005). Teacher judgments—going beyond criteria for judging performance. *Babel*, 39(3), 8–16.

Stobart, G. (2008). *Testing times the uses and abuses of assessment.* London, Routledge.

Suto, W.M.I. & Greatorex, J. (2008). A quantitative analysis of cognitive strategy usage in the marking of two GCSE examinations. *Assessment in Education: Principles, Policy & Practice.*, 15 (1), 73–89.

Wenger, E. (1998). *Communities of practice. learning, meaning and identity.* Cambridge, Cambridge University Press.

Wyatt-Smith, C. & Klenowski, V. (2012). Explicit, latent and meta-criteria: types of criteria at play in professional judgement practice. *Assessment in Education: Principles, Policy & Practice.* Available online at: http://www.tandfonline.com/action/showAxaArticles?journalCode= caie20

Wyatt-Smith, C., Klenowski, V. & Gunn, S. (2010). The centrality of teachers' judgement practice in assessment: a study of standards in moderation. *Assessment in Education: Principles, Policy and Practice*, 17(1), 59–75.

The public understanding of assessment in educational reform in the United States

Susan M. Brookhart

Duquesne University and Brookhart Enterprises LLC, USA

The United States education system depends on legislation and funding at the federal, state and local levels. Public understanding of assessment therefore is important to educational reform in the USA. Educational reformers often invoke assessment information as a reason for reform, typically by citing unacceptable achievement on some measure or indicator. Recent educational reforms in the US also rely on assessment information as evidence of the effectiveness of the reform, designing some sort of accountability system into the reform. Public opinion about testing in three recent waves of US educational reform (the minimum competency movement in the 1970s, the standards-based reform movement in the 1980s and 1990s, and the No Child Left Behind era beginning in 2002) shows two themes. One is public belief in the objectivity of testing. The other is public belief in using tests data comparatively and competitively.

Introduction

The United States (US) education system depends on legislation and funding at the federal, state and local levels. Educational reformers often both invoke assessment information as a reason for reform and also rely on assessment information for evidence of the effectiveness of the reform. Therefore, public understanding of assessment is a critical element in US educational reform.

Purpose and method

This paper analyses the measurement, educational and social issues involved in the public understanding of assessment evidenced in three recent waves of US educational reform: the minimum competency movement in the 1970s, the standards-based reform movement in the 1980s and 1990s, and the No Child Left Behind (NCLB) era beginning in 2002. Since standardised tests have been the assessments most used in these reform movements, most of the public attitudes described in this paper are attitudes toward testing.

The paper begins by describing two themes that can be seen throughout all three educational reform movements. The first, mechanical objectivity, is not unique to the US but is evidenced in all parts of the developed world that rely on science and technology and conduct commerce across jurisdictions. The second, a valuing of economic success and competition in all realms, may not be unique to the US but is certainly exemplified in much US education rhetoric.

The next section describes the development of public understanding of assessment in the US. Before the minimum competency testing movement in the 1970s, testing and assessment were not salient in the mind of the public or of policymakers, but remained the purview of educators. Three subsections treat the minimum competency testing movement, the standards-based reform movement, and the No Child Left Behind era, respectively. A final section draws conclusions about the current and future public understanding of assessment in the US.

Setting the stage

Mechanical objectivity

The importance of numbers, public trust in numbers, and the illusion of mechanical objectivity is the subject of Porter's (1995) *Trust in numbers*. Porter shows that standardisation of measures arose from economic and social needs, for example the need for a standard bushel as communities began to trade with each other.

With the rise of mathematics and scientific methods, and the rise of political democracy and thus the need to defend bureaucratic decisions to outsiders, both the public and policy makers have come to rely more and more on the perceived rigour of mathematics and 'mechanical objectivity'. Mechanical objectivity means following the rules (Porter, 1995, p. 4), although in reality pure mechanical objectivity is an illusion. No data or decisions are completely devoid of any contextual knowledge, for example deciding what to measure and why. Yet once numbers exist, they give the illusion that a rigorous and fair process has been followed (Porter, 1995, p. 8) because mathematical procedures will crank out the same answers for the same data. For example, once a cut score is set on an assessment, one passes or fails accordingly, and the examiner does not have to decide. Porter (1995, p. 9) put it this way: 'Scientific objectivity thus provides an answer to a moral demand for impartiality and fairness. Quantification is a way of making decisions without seeming to decide. Objectivity lends authority to officials who have very little of their own.' This perspective is not unique to the US. It is, however, important background for recent and current US public attitudes toward assessment.

In the US, at least from the early 1900s in some fields (e.g., accounting and engineering), faith in scientific objectivity blossomed. In education, faith in the 'new science of testing' began to develop, through the work of E. L. Thorndike and others, in the early 1900s. Progressive educators began to use external standardised testing as a way to demonstrate the ineffectiveness of old-fashioned schooling (Gamson, 2007, p. 23). A movement towards collecting systematic, scientific evidence of the results of education became known as 'the new science of education'.

However, the 'new science' of educational testing remained mostly the province of educational evaluators, researchers and psychologists. It would be the 1970s before the general public developed an interest in the outcomes of schooling as measured by tests (Dorn, 1998). Given the public trust in numbers, it was a short leap from the rise of interest in the outcomes of schooling to the use of test scores as instruments of mechanical objectivity.

The public understanding of test scores as instruments of mechanical objectivity is the first theme of this article. McDonnell (2005) pointed out that policymakers and constituents must believe in the myth of objectivity when they make judgments about schools and individuals where rewards and sanctions are applied or winners and losers are created. They must believe that their decisions are based on valid and unbiased information and that therefore they are being objective and fair-minded. Even if policymakers could be convinced of the limits of testing, they would need to replace the myth that tests are objective with an equally powerful myth, 'because policymaking is about persuasion, and myths persuade. Whether such a replacement myth can even be found and whatever it might be, it would have to serve the same public function—namely, facilitating the political accountability of schools and allocating scarce resources in a seemingly fair and impartial way' (McDonnell, 2005, p. 49).

Competition and economic thinking

One of the properties of numbers is that they can be ordered, by mathematical rules that on the face of it seem rigorous, to create a competition with winners and losers. As Dorn (1998) observed: 'The production and presentation of statistics is part of the fabric of public debate, and public policy that involves the heavy use of statistics must consider the long-term consequences of that use.' Once again, what is seemingly mechanical is based on the values of those who select, analyse and use the numbers.

The rise of public interest in the outcomes of education and the concomitant growing interest in test scores to indicate those outcomes was showcased in an important domestic competition in US education in the 1950s, between proponents of segregation and proponents of desegregation. The desegregation of schools in the wake of the 1954 US Supreme Court decision *Brown vs Board of Education of Topeka* declared unconstitutional the policy of maintaining separate public school systems for black and white students (Diner, 1982; Dorn, 1998). Both sides used test scores to support their position. For example, as the Washington DC public schools desegregated, proponents of segregation used poor test score data to argue that integrating the schools led to bad outcomes, and proponents of desegregation used poor test score data to argue that culturally disadvantaged children had been poorly served by the unequal school system in which they had been raised (Diner, 1982, pp. 27–28).

This paper takes up the US minimum competency movement in the 1970, where economic competitions (competitions, that is, in the mind of the public) have largely, although not completely, replaced other competitions around test scores. The most important perceived domestic competition in US education today is shown in the ranking of schools, districts, teachers and students to support economic winners and losers. For example, the quality of a local school district's education, as measured by its performance on standardised tests, can affect the real estate property values in the district. The most important perceived international competition is shown in the reactions to US rankings on international standardised tests and the slippery-slope logic used to draw conclusions about the ability to compete and win in the global economic market (Kirst, 1985; Cavanaugh, 2007, 2012). This perceived function of test scores representing economic value and competitiveness is a second theme of this article.

Development of public understanding of assessment in the United States

From the beginning of the interest in standardised testing in the US, tests were used for two different purposes: sorting and selecting students, and evaluating and improving educational quality. Both of these purposes were evident to educators from the beginning of the 20th century (Haertel & Herman, 2005). However, student achievement as the major 'output' of schooling did not capture the public attention until the middle of the 20th century. Public interest in assessment of student learning outcomes awakened in the 1970s, at the beginning of what is now three waves of outcomes-referenced educational reform.

Prior to that, the public interest in education centered on the 'inputs' of schooling, like buildings and grounds, business management and school governance, student/teacher ratios, and the like (Diner, 1982). The first major federal legislation to require testing programmes in the context of federal funding was the National Defense Education Act (NDEA) (Gamson, 2007) in 1958. The NDEA required schools that wanted federal funds to have a programme of testing in secondary schools to identify the best course of study for students' abilities and to identify students with outstanding aptitudes and abilities so they could prepare for college. The role of testing in schooling thus expanded, but still on the input side.

Even then, testing was not at the top of the public's consciousness. The first national television news broadcasts about standardised test score levels occurred on ABC and CBS on October 28, 1975 (Dorn, 1998), in the middle of what would come to be called the minimum competency testing movement. Figure 1 presents a timeline of US events influencing public and policy uses of test scores for the achievement outcomes of schooling.

Figure 1 shows seminal events and legislation that presaged and helped develop an emphasis on the outcomes of schooling, and then seminal events and legislation that occurred in each of the three waves of reform in which testing and assessment of the outcomes of schooling figured prominently. These three waves of reform were the minimum competency testing movement, the standards-based reform movement, and the No Child Left Behind era, respectively.

Each section below begins with a description of the respective reform movement and its historical context. Next, evidence about public attitudes toward testing at the time is presented, from the *Annual Phi Delta Kappa/Gallup Poll of the Public's Attitude Toward the Public Schools*. This survey began in 1969 and is currently in its 44th year. The survey is valuable for its nationally representative sample, for its longitudinal and ongoing picture of public attitudes, and as a mirror of what has been on the public's mind in different years. The questions asked each year reflect the current 'hot topics' and public concerns in education. All 44 surveys were reviewed; this article presents only results about public attitudes toward testing and assessment. Finally, each section contains an analysis of the measurement, educational and social issues apparent in the reform movement's treatment of testing and assessment and in the public's attitudes.

The minimum competency testing movement

Beginning in the late 1960s and continuing into the 1970s, public concern arose over declines in standardised test scores (Waters, 1981) and high unemployment among young people. The public became disenchanted with the public schools. A 'back to the basics' movement arose, which held that students were being passed from grade to grade without learning 'the basics' (e.g., reading, writing and arithmetic), that schools should teach these basics and cut back on 'frills'. For the first time in a major way, public emphasis switched to educational outcomes (Haertel & Herman, 2005).

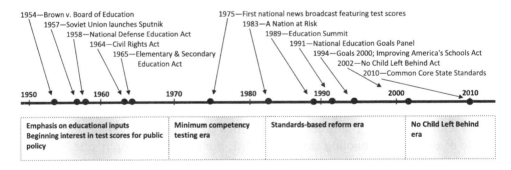

Figure 1.   Time line of US events influencing public policy uses of test scores

Writing up the results of the 1977 *Gallup poll of the public's attitude toward the public school*, Gallup (1977, p. 36) asserted: 'The decline in national test scores and frequent media reports of illiteracy among high school graduates have given impetus to what is now widely referred to as the back-to-basics movement.' Forty-one percent of a nationally representative sample of the public said they had heard or read about the back-to-basics movement; of those familiar with the term, 83% approved of the movement (Gallup, 1977, p. 37).

Test scores gained the limelight as the public began to value them as objective measures of educational outcomes. Using what seemed like logical thinking, the public looked to outcome test scores to validate school reforms put in place as a response to a decline in scores on valued tests like the SAT and ACT admission tests taken by college-bound high school students. Outcomes-oriented curriculum reforms associated with the minimum competency testing movement went by names like Competency-Based Curriculum (Diner, 1982), Competency-Based Education (Branch & Walters, 1981) and, later, a more controversial version called Outcomes Based Education that extended outcomes beyond academic achievement into values and attitudes, and thus beyond what some considered the bounds of public schooling (O'Neill, 1994).

The idea behind minimum competency testing was that students would have to pass a basic skills test to graduate from high school, and by 1980 29 states had minimum competency requirements (Haertel & Herman, 2005). Support-ers of the minimum competency testing movement cited 'kids buckling down and getting serious about their school work' (Frahm & Covington, 1979, p. 48). Critics called it a 'cheap fix on a serious problem' and a 'new fad' (Frahm & Covington, 1979, p. 44). Concerns included a worry that in order for pass rates to be high enough to be politically acceptable, passing scores would be set inordinately low; concerns about discrimination and effects on students of colour and students in poverty; and the problem of scale and expense, with money used for testing diminishing money available for instruc-tional resources.

Public attitudes. The first Gallup survey of the public's attitudes toward the public schools, in 1969, did not report asking any testing questions. In six of the 10 polls during the 1970s, however, the poll did ask questions about public perceptions of testing.

During this era, a large majority of the public supported the use of tests as objective measures of student achievement. This finding supports the theme of a public desire for mechanical objectivity (Porter, 1995), a wish for a simple and clear indicator of educational quality. Sixty-five percent of the public in 1976 thought high school students should be required to pass a standard examination in order to get a high school diploma, compared with 50% in 1958 (Gallup, 1976, p. 199). Sixty-eight percent of the public in 1978 thought children should be promoted from grade to grade only if they could pass examinations (Gallup, 1978, p. 36).

In addition, public opinion in the 1970s supported the 'competition' theme in that the public wanted measures that allowed comparisons among students. In both 1970 and 1971, the Gallup poll asked the question: 'Would you like to see the students in the local schools be given national tests so that their educational achievement could be compared with students in other communities?' (Gallup, 1970, p. 106). A majority of respondents said Yes (75% in 1970 and 70% in 1971; Gallup, 1971, p. 43). When asked whether they would prefer to see tests prepared on a local, state or national level, there was more support for local (37%) than state (25%) or national (28%) test development (Gallup, 1978, p. 37).

Public opinion in the 1970s also documented concerns over the declining national test scores, and especially the SAT tests taken by college-bound high school seniors. The poll asked an open question to ascertain public perceptions of the reasons for the decline. The majority answers included (Gallup, 1975, p. 235): students' lack of interest/motivation (29%); lack of discipline at home and in school (28%); poor curriculum (too easy, not enough emphasis on basics) (22%); and inadequate or uninterested teachers (21%). Fifty-nine percent of the public believed that a decline in national test scores meant the quality of education was declining (Gallup, 1976, p. 199).

Measurement, educational, and social issues. Public attitudes during the minimum competency tests movement raise measurement, educational and social issues. The main measurement issue in the story of the movement above is a validity issue. Tests are theoretically conceived of as a collection of items or tasks that sample from a domain. Inferences are made from a student's performance on the items to an observed score, from the observed score to an expected score in the universe of generalisation, from there to the target score or expected value over the whole domain, and from there to a verbal description interpreting student's capabilities (Kane, 2006). Some error is associated with each inference.

In contrast, the public's belief in testing requirements in basic skills and the belief that declining test scores meant a decline in educational quality suggest that the public reifies test scores, treating them as a kind of 'reality'. The simplicity of public opinion suggests that many do not make the distinction between concrete measurements (inches, pounds, dollars) and mental measurements and do not understand the inferences that must be made in testing and the probabilistic nature of test information. This is in line with the theme of mechanical objectivity and demonstrates a perceived need for a simple and fairly concrete indicator for education.

During the minimum competency testing movement, the main educational issue was the choice of what to test, namely basic skills. Maintaining expectations for students that carried sanctions like high school graduation, and yet also maintaining the principle that these expectations were minimums, proved difficult. If passing a minimum competency basic skills test is the hurdle one has to aim to clear in order to graduate from high school, it is easy for basic skills to become the goal. A saying at the time went: 'The minimum becomes the maximum.'

The minimum competency testing movement raised at least two social issues. One was the spectre of competition, one of the themes of this article. The finding that the public wants an objective measure that specifically can be used to compare schools is robust across the decade. Public comparisons in the newspaper and on television—at the time there was no internet—resulted in labeling some schools, students and parents as winners and others as losers. This is, perhaps, appealing to those who expect to be winners, and some believe that competition creates a 'horse-race' mentality where people will try hard to win. Even if this is true for some, however, it is only true for those who have at least a slim chance of winning. There is also the mathematical reality of ranking that, no matter how excellent everyone's performance is, ranking still creates losers. Again, this bespeaks at least some potential winners with little regard for fairness to others as long as their own supremacy is established. A US aphorism sums up this attitude: 'Looking out for number one.'

A second social issue is apparent in the public's opinions about why test scores had been declining from the late 1960s through the 1970s. In the top responses, one seems to hear a bit of 'blame the victim'. The two most frequent responses were about uninterested, undisciplined and unmotivated students—blaming students for their lack of accomplishment. The third and fourth most frequent responses blamed poor curriculum and poor teachers—blaming educators for their lack of accomplishment. While a very few responses did mention more general social ills, none of the responses depicted a social system of moving parts that were not working well together. As with the public need for a simple, objective measure for evaluation, it seems a majority of the public also wants simple reasons for failure, and blaming the victim is one of the simplest.

The Standards-based reform movement

By the end of the 1970s, public interest in improving education and remediating youth social problems (crime, addiction, teen pregnancy) remained high, but the available test score evidence did not produce a resounding endorsement for minimum competency testing (Lerner, 1982). The minimum competency testing movement faded (OTA, 1992). Public concern shifted from minimum competency in basic skills to higher standards and assessments that required higher-order thinking skills and complex performances.

In 1983, a national commission published *A Nation at Risk* (NCEE, 1983), a widely influential document that proclaimed US students were falling behind. The report used some incendiary rhetoric designed to appeal simultaneously to the public's fears and to national pride: 'If an unfriendly foreign power had attempted to impose on America the mediocre educational performance that exists today, we might well have viewed it as an act of war' (NCEE, 1983). The report advocated rigorous and measurable standards and high expectations, a commitment to both excellence and equity, and recommended state and local use of standardised achievement tests. Most states responded by creating state content and performance standards and mandating student achievement testing (Dotterweich & McNeal, 2003; Gamson, 2007).

The educational reform movement of the 1980s and 1990s became known as the 'standards movement' (Porter, 1993). As for the minimum competency testing movement, student assessment was used for monitoring outcomes, but the outcomes were seen as high standards rather than basic skills.

States and the federal government were both involved in the movement. Each state developed its own state content and performance standards and student assessments. At the federal level, President George H. W. Bush brought state governors together for an Education Summit in 1989. The governors agreed on six broad goals for American students to reach by the year 2000, which led to the formation of the National Educational Goals Panel in 1991 and, in 1994 during the administration of President Clinton, the *Goals 2000: Educate America Act*, which provided funding for states to work on creating challenging academic standards.

All six goals set expectations for which assessments were needed. Two in particular fuelled the development of assessment of academic achievement (NEGP, 1991). Goal 3 specified that students would 'leave grades 4, 8, and 12 having demonstrated competency in challenging subject matter.' Goal 4 specified that by 2000, US students would be 'first in the world in science and mathematics.' Congress debated, but decided against, developing national tests in reading and mathematics because there was resistance to 'nationalising' education (Cortez, 1998).

During this era, the idea of educational accountability based on assessing student achievement of standards became firmly entrenched in the public's mind. As Joseph Spagnolo (1997, p. 7), then Illinois State Superintendent of Education, said: 'I have a legislator that pounds on the table and says we're not going to give you any more money until you give us accountability.'

In addition to the ubiquitous multiple-choice tests, states experimented with various performance assessments and portfolios. Vermont, Kentucky, California and Maryland were known for statewide assessment systems that included performance assessments. Reliability (Koretz *et al.*, 1994) and cost became issues for large-scale performance assessment. However, states did achieve some measure of success with these assessments (Hambleton *et al.*, 2000). None of these performance assessments are in use currently, having given way to the state assessments used under the No Child Left Behind Act.

Public attitudes. The Gallup poll reported responses to questions about testing students in 14 of the 22 polls from 1980 through 2001. In many of the poll reports, testing questions took more space and were more prominently written up than in the reports in the 1970s. This suggests that those who conducted the poll thought testing questions were becoming more important in the mind of the public.

The theme of mechanical objectivity is evident in public support for a national test for high school graduation (69% in 1981 and 65% in 1984) and support for state board examinations for teachers (84% in 1981 and 89% in 1984) (Gallup, 1984, pp. 31–32). Other questions about testing students for promotion and graduation and testing teachers for certification during these decades of standards-based reform garnered high support as well (Elam, 1990; Elam *et al.*, 1992, 1994; Rose & Gallup, 2000, 2001).

The theme of competition and comparison within the US loomed large during the decades of the standards-based reform movement, and in the poll itself:

> In his 1984 State of the Union Address, President Reagan asserted, 'Just as more incentives are needed within our schools, greater competition is needed among our schools. Without standards and competition there can be no champions, no records broken, no excellence—in education or any other walk of life.' The public agrees. Seventy percent favour reporting the results of achievement tests by state and by school, so that comparisons can be made. The public feels that such comparisons would serve as incentives to local public schools, whether the results showed higher or lower scores for students. (Gallup & Clark, 1987, p. 18)

During this era, support grew for achievement testing and making comparisons. The basic question about testing and reporting on a state-by-state and school-by-school basis so comparisons can be made was asked in several years. Table 1 presents data over all the years that the poll asked the general question about support for national testing and comparisons of the results.

The 1987 poll asked public opinion about using tests to compare schools, whether this opinion held if local results were higher or lower than other schools' scores, and whether local schools would interpret test score comparisons as an incentive (72% said yes) (Gallup & Clark, 1987, p. 19).

The theme of international competition and comparison was evident in a special set of questions asked in the 1996 poll. Elam *et al.* (1996, p. 57) reported that, even given the controversial nature of ranking countries with very different cultures, school systems and samples, 69% of the public believed mathematics achievement was lower in the US than in other developed countries, and 54% believed reading achievement was lower.

One of the reasons that the national goals movement was able to grow was public support for the idea. In 1989, 70% of the public favoured national achievement standards and goals (Elam & Gallup, 1989, p. 44), and 77%

Table 1. Responses from a nationally representative sample to the question: Would you like to see the students in the local schools be given national tests, so that their educational achievement could be compared with students in other communities?

Percent who answered	1970	1971	1983	1986	1988
Yes	75	70	75	77	81
No	17	21	17	16	14
Don't know	8	9	8	7	5

Source: Annual Phi Delta Kappa/Gallup Survey of the Public's Attitudes Toward the Public Schools

favoured requiring schools in the community to use standardised national testing programmes to measure that achievement (p. 45). In 1991, the same 77% favoured testing, and support was even stronger when the question was asked more specifically: 88% favoured standardised national tests in core subjects, 84% in problem-solving, and 85% in writing (Elam *et al.*, 1991, p. 44).

Higher standards for academic achievement also had broad public support. By the mid-1990s, most states had drafted standards. However, the movement was beginning to stir controversy as questions arose like who should set standards, would they really be for all students, and would students have access to the instruction needed to achieve them. Nevertheless, in 1995, 87% of the public favoured higher standards, even if it meant fewer students would graduate from high school (65%; Elam & Rose, 1995, p. 47).

Toward the end of the standards-based reform era, some concern arose that US students might be subject to too much testing. In 2001, 31% of the public agreed there was too much emphasis on standardised testing (similar to 30% in 2000 and up from 20% in 1997), although the majority (44%) thought there was just the right amount of emphasis on testing (Rose and Gallup, 2001, p. 53).

There was also some indication that the public, although supporting standardised testing, was beginning to see its main usefulness as an input of instruction rather than an outcome. In 2000, when asked whether the primary purpose of tests should be to determine how much the students have learned or to determine the kind of instruction needed, 30% of the public said determine learning—the outcome—and 65% said determine instruction—the input (Rose & Gallup, 2000, p. 53). In both 2000 and 2001, when asked the best way to measure student academic achievement, 68% and 65%, respectively, said classroom work and homework, compared with 26% and 31%, respectively, who said test scores (Rose & Gallup, 2001, p. 54). Shepard & Bleim (1995) found similar results in their survey of parents in three schools, who said they found talking with their child's teacher the most useful source of information about their child's academic progress.

These national percentages may mask group differences. Political scientists Dotterweich and McNeal analysed January 2001 CBS News monthly poll data, which was collected as the standards-based reform movement was giving way to what at the time were President George W. Bush's election promises related to NCLB. They found that individuals (a) in states with higher minority diversity, (b) in states with fewer initiatives on the ballot, (c) in states that did not currently use mandatory testing for high school graduation, (d) who were Republican, (e) who were male, and (f) who had fewer children were more likely to favour mandatory testing (Dotterweich & McNeal, 2003, p. 17).

Measurement, educational, and social issues. Public attitudes during the standards-based reform era raise some of the same issues as public attitudes during the minimum competency tests movement. Some issues intensified, and some new issues arose.

The main measurement issues were, as in the 1970s, about validity. The theme of mechanical objectivity and the measurement issue of not understanding mental measurements as based on samples of performance and requiring a string of inferences are, if anything, intensified in the strong public support for qualification-type tests for graduation, promotion and teacher certification. Clearly the public at large saw test scores as analogous to 'yardsticks' for measuring achievement.

A second validity issue seems to lurk in the public's somewhat two-faced responses, giving strong support to testing for graduation, promotion and certification and yet also saying the most important use of test scores is for diagnosing student learning needs. A test that is good for graduation and promotion will, of necessity, have to sample lightly from a broad array of educational goals. Such a test will not yield enough fine-grained information about student understanding of any one of them to determine instruction. A test that does yield such information will, of necessity, have a lot of items on a relatively narrow set of goals, to find out where the student is and his or her specific needs regarding those goals. The public seems to think of 'tests' as a unitary concept. Not understanding that there are many kinds of tests and that each serves some purposes and not others risks potential public support of misuses of tests.

The educational issues apparent in the standards-based reform era were a result of the backlash against the minimum competencies that became maximums during the previous reform movement. The challenging content required by higher standards moved education forward but required assessments that more or less fell of their own weight. Challenging content is harder to measure than basic skills, and expensive. Challenging tasks are more difficult to write than basic skills items. They take time for students to do, and for accurate measurement students need to complete many different tasks. Most such tasks required human scoring, which in turn required time and training. The 'standards' movement had the dubious distinction of being educationally more sound than the previous movement but practically more difficult. Efficiency and cost ultimately won out in the case of most of the ambitious assessment experiments associated with the standards-based reform era.

The major social issue for assessment in the standards-based reform era was again competition among schools, this time intensified by an order of magnitude. Fuelled by the 'no excellence without competition' rhetoric of President Reagan and many others, newspaper rankings of school districts became common. Fear and embarrassment for schools that did not show well in these comparisons was rampant. This social issue, of schools needing to best each other, in turn fed back into the educational and measurement issues. Many schools were left caring more about how they fared on state tests, compared with their neighboring districts, than about student learning. In turn, this affected both their views of tests and the education in classrooms.

The No Child Left Behind (NCLB) era

The No Child Left Behind Act of 2001 was signed into law in January 2002. It is, at the time of this writing, the most recent re-authorisation of the 1965 Elementary and Secondary Education Act (ESEA). NCLB contained many of the same provisions as the original ESEA legislation. Three new emphases were added (student testing, high quality teachers and research-based programmes) (NCLB, 2002). The requirement for annual testing of all students in grades 3 to 8 and once in high school received the most attention from both educators and the public.

NCLB provided that states must report to the federal government the percentage of students who were proficient in reading and mathematics (and subsequently science), disaggregate those results by subgroup (poverty, minority status, English proficiency, disabilities), and make 'adequate yearly progress' toward proficiency for all students by 2014. Sanctions with high stakes for schools were invoked for schools that failed to make adequate yearly progress two years in a row. As 2014 draws closer, more and more schools have failed to make adequate yearly progress, and there is currently some flexibility in the sanctions (see www2.ed.gov/nclb/ for details).

As with previous federal education legislation going back at least to the Individuals with Disabilities Education Act of 1975, policy makers as well as the public respond to federal regulation of education, which in the US is constitutionally a state function, with two opposing perspectives. Some hold that such federal regulation is interfering in a state function. Others support the federal activism in attempting to improve the lives of students (Ramanathan, 2008). Because NCLB regulations were so comprehensive, responses to NCLB from both these camps has been strong.

NCLB is generally credited with both negative and positive results. On the negative side, there is some evidence that curriculum and instruction have narrowed in local attempts to teach to the test (Au, 2007) and that many teachers, although not necessarily parents, perceive there is too much testing (Johnson *et al.*, 2006). On the positive side, the disaggregation requirement has shone a light on the performance of previously overlooked groups (Jennings & Rentner, 2006) and raised awareness of their needs and schools' responses to them.

Public attitudes. The Gallup poll reported responses to questions about testing students in every poll from 2002 to 2010, and in 2012. Most poll questions specifically mentioned NCLB. NCLB had such expanded testing requirements, compared with anything that had gone before, that opinions about the law and testing were seen as related. In 2002, the year NCLB became law, 67% favoured the tracking of student progress from grades 3 to 8 based on an annual test, and 96% favoured a statewide subject-matter competency test for teachers (Rose & Gallup, 2002, p. 45). Public support of tracking student progress using standardised tests continued through the decade (66% favourable in 2009) (Bushaw & McNee, 2009, p. 12).

However, when the details of NCLB were held up for scrutiny, the public did not support some of them. In 2003, 84% of the public believed whether students showed reasonable improvement from where they started was the better way to judge how a public school is doing, rather than current achievement status (the original NCLB requirement), and 66% (67% in 2004) believed a single test would not provide a fair picture of whether a school needed improvement (Rose & Gallup, 2003, p. 45; 2004, p. 46). At that time, 66% of the public believed NCLB's heavy emphasis on standardised tests would encourage teaching to the tests rather than teaching the subject (Rose & Gallup, 2003, p. 46).

In 2004 and 2005, the poll contained an expanded section of questions about NCLB. In 2005 the percentage of the public that thought there was too much testing rose to 36%, up from 31% at the end of the standards-based reform era (Rose & Gallup, 2005, p. 47). Public opinion was split, with slightly more in favour, over whether one of the measures of teachers' (52% yes, 44% no) and principals' (50% yes, 46% no) performance quality should be based on their students' standardised test scores. Equivocating about whether there was too much testing continued throughout the decade. Table 2 presents all available poll data on this question, from the end of the standards-based reform era and throughout the first decade of the 21st century and the NCLB era.

In 2007, after presenting responses to a set of questions about the amount of and emphasis on testing and the phenomenon of teaching to the test, Rose and Gallup (2007, p. 37) concluded: 'What the data say to us is that the public is growing disenchanted with the growing reliance on standardised testing. It seems likely that there is no coincidence in the fact that the criticism of standardised testing has developed since standardised testing became the principal strategy in implementing NCLB.'

Writing for Public Agenda, a public opinion research organisation, Johnson et al. (2006) interpreted this phenomenon a bit differently. Their opinion polls led them to conclude (p. 1), 'there is strong belief in the intrinsic value of

Table 2. Responses from a nationally representative sample to the question: In your opinion, is there too much emphasis on achievement testing in the public schools in your community, not enough emphasis on testing, or about the right amount?

Percent who answered	1997	2000	2001	2002	2004	2005	2006	2007	2008
Too much	20	30	31	31	32	36	39	43	37
Not enough	28	23	22	19	22	17	25	15	23
About right	48	43	44	47	40	40	33	40	34
Don't know	4	4	3	3	6	7	3	2	6

Source: Annual Phi Delta Kappa/Gallup Survey of the Public's Attitudes Toward the Public Schools

standards and testing and broad support for key elements such as high school exit exams.' Rather, their polls indicated, other issues like student behaviour, motivation and cooperation were more urgent than standards and testing, and the use of a single test for high-stakes decisions was not supported (Johnson & Duffett, 2003; Johnson et al., 2006). Their data also indicated that teachers were more concerned than parents about the amount of testing (71% of teachers said their students took too many tests, compared with 17% of parents) (Johnson et al., 2006, p. 17).

Measurement, educational, and social issues. Public attitudes during the No Child Left Behind era continued to embody the themes of the objectivity of testing and the usefulness of tests as indicators for economic competitiveness. An additional public concern arose as even the US public, desirous of bottom-line accountability measures, began to wonder if there was too much testing.

The measurement issues continued to be validity issues. The public continued to see test scores as objective things, holding schools and perhaps educators responsible for scores as if they were a form of currency. However, the public did evidence some intuitive validity-like reasoning. Public opinion reacted against the original NCLB requirement to report achievement status, as opposed to growth, for school accountability. It seemed logical that the right construct for which to hold schools accountable was how far students came under their tutelage, rather than student achievement status regardless of starting point. Additionally, there was public concern for making high-stakes decisions on the basis of just one test. There is not enough evidence to say whether this is a sort of intuitive validity reasoning, reliability reasoning, or just the public's tiring of the largely expanded use of state standardised testing under NCLB.

The main educational issue certainly was the sheer weight of states' programmes of accountability testing under NCLB. Educators, more than any other group, perceived accountability tests to be the tail wagging the dog. Concerns included narrowing of curriculum and teaching to the test as well as more practical concerns like the sheer amount of time and energy required for testing and, in some cases, educators' feeling that students' future performance on an accountability test was always hanging over their heads. This, of course, is the result that legislators and the public, who saw tests as bottom-line measures, wanted, but when it arrived it was uncomfortable to educators and dampened their enthusiasm and their work environment.

The main social issue under accountability testing in the NCLB era continued to be competition. School-level data in various forms was (and is) available for public consumption on most state department of education websites. Sometimes it is in the form of lists that tell which schools met adequate yearly progress for NCLB accountability. Sometimes school 'report cards' present more detailed data about reading and mathematics, and sometimes science, test results. It is easy to find out how one's local school fared in comparison with others in the school district and state and to identify winners and losers.

Current and future public understanding of assessment in the United States

Those in the measurement community are often concerned about the public's understanding of assessment and wish that the public had a more nuanced understanding of what test scores mean, including viewing them as a sample of performances in a domain, subject to measurement error, that yield imperfect but useful scores on abstract mental processes that cannot be observed directly. As Linn (1993, p. 1) observed: 'Educational assessments are often rather naively expected to serve the role of a kind of impartial barometer of educational quality. Such an expectation makes assessment results of particular interest and value to policymakers of various stripes.'

The information and analyses in this paper suggest that is true as far as it goes, but that test scores do serve some public purposes that go beyond simply the public's misunderstanding of assessment or lack of assessment literacy. A case has been made that treating test scores as bottom-line, concrete indicators of educational quality—a public understanding so powerful that McDonnell (2005) has called it a myth—serves at least two public purposes. First, it allows for treating test scores in a mechanically objective way, which absolves politicians, policy makers, and the general public from any guilt or shame or charges of bias in decision-making. Second, it serves as a yardstick in a competition that will tell who has won the race. This view fits well with the current public understanding of education as a race for economic competitiveness. Such a competitive spirit about education has been in evidence at least since 1957, when the Soviet Union launched Sputnik I, the world's first artificial satellite, into space and fired a competition that came to be called the Space Race (Cavanaugh, 2007). In current economic times, the public's understanding of test scores as bottom-line indicators of educational quality is usually construed to indicate economic competitiveness.

If these theses are truthful, then increasing public assessment literacy is not, in and of itself, a strategy that will bring the public understanding of assessment more in line with the wishes of measurement experts. Increasing public assessment literacy is an important goal, and the current climate of high-stakes testing may provide the best opportunity in a long time to pursue that goal because the topic is salient. However, other strategies will be needed to meet the US public's clearly felt need for some sort of aid to decision making and yardstick in various social races. More difficult, strategies to make US society less competitive might be pursued.

Such strategies are obviously out of reach, and the next generation of US outcomes-oriented educational reforms is beginning with a different premise. That premise is that better standards and better assessment will make for better information about education quality and better decisions. On June 2, 2010, the National Governors Association Center for Best Practices and the Council of Chief State School Officers released a set of state-led education standards called the Common Core State Standards, for English language arts and mathematics.

One of the claims made by the developers is that these standards, 'Are informed by other top performing countries, so that all students are prepared to succeed in our global economy and society (www.corestandards.org). The Common Core State Standards differ somewhat from most existing state content standards, in both topic coverage and cognitive demand (Porter *et al.*, 2011). States that adopt the Common Core State Standards (at this writing, 45 states out of 50) agree to use them as at least 85% of their state standards.

On 2 September 2010, the US Secretary of Education announced two winners in a federal grant competition to the Partnership for Assessment of Readiness for College and Careers (PARCC, currently with 24 states involved) and the SMARTER Balanced Assessment Consortium (currently with 27 states involved). Some states are involved in both consortia, and a few are affiliated with neither. One of the major avowed purposes of this new test development is to make better tests, including harnessing the most sophisticated measurement theory and using the new assessment resources computers can offer.

The expectation for better tests was made explicitly to the US public:

> 'As I travel around the country the number one complaint I hear from teachers is that state bubble tests pressure teachers to teach to a test that doesn't measure what really matters,' said [US Secretary of Education] Duncan. 'Both of these winning applicants are planning to develop assessments that will move us far beyond this and measure real student knowledge and skills.' (http://www.ed.gov/news/press-releases/us-secretary-edu-cation-duncan-announces-winners-competition-improve-student-asse)

Both PARCC and the SMARTER Balanced Assessment Consortium are busy developing requests for proposals and letting contracts. Both consortia plan to have operational tests available for use in the 2014–2015 school year. As work begins, and as the time for implementation of the new assessments draws closer, there will soon be evidence of whether the US and the two assessment consortia and their affiliated states have reached the goal of better assessments for better standards. Of course, they will still be tests and subject to the validity issues described above. But they may be better tests than current state assessments. For now, all that can be concluded definitively is that, as utopian as the goal of 'better tests' sounds, it has a greater chance of success than changing the public myth of the objectivity of assessment and of its usefulness as an educational bottom line.

References

Au, W. (2007). High-stakes testing and curricular control: A qualitative metasynthesis. *Educational Researcher*, 36, 258–267.

Branch, J.S. & Walters, E. (1981). Competency-based approach: assessing effectiveness: a transitional study. *NASSP Bulletin*, 65, 40–43.

Bushaw, W.J. & McNee, J.A. (2009). The 41st Annual Phi Delta Kappa/Gallup poll of the public's attitudes toward the public schools—Americans speak out: are educators and policy makers listening? *Phi Delta Kappan*, 91(1), 8–23.

Cavanaugh, S. (2007, September 26). Lessons drawn from Sputnik 50 years later. *Education Week*, 27(5), 1–14.

Cavanaugh, S. (2012, January 12). US Education pressured by international comparisons. *Education Week*. Available online at: http://www.edweek.org/ew/articles/2012/01/12/16overview.h31.html?qs=international+comparisons (accessed 30 April 2012).

Cortez, A. (1998, September). Standards, assessments and accountability. IDRA Newsletter, 25 (8), 3–4. ERIC Document No. ED 423 103.

Diner, S. J. (1982, May). *Crisis of confidence. the reputation of Washington's public schools in the twentieth century*. Studies in DC History and Public Policy Paper No. 1. ERIC Document No. 218 374. Washington, Department of Urban Studies, University of DC.

Dorn, S. (1998). The political legacy of school accountability systems. *Education Policy Analysis Archives*, 6(1). Available online at: http://epaa.asu.edu/ojs/.

Dotterweich, L. & McNeal, R. (2003). The No Child Left Behind Act and public preferences. Paper presented at the *Annual Meeting of the American Political Science Association*, Philadelphia. ERIC Document No. DC 479 757.

Elam, S.M. (1990). The 22nd annual Phi Delta Kappa/Gallup poll of the public's attitude toward the public schools. *Phi Delta Kappan*, 72(1), 41–55.

Elam, S.M. & Gallup, A.M. (1989). The 21st annual Phi Delta Kappa/Gallup poll of the public's attitude toward the public schools. *Phi Delta Kappan*, 71(1), 41–54.

Elam, S.M. & Rose, L.C. (1995). The 27th annual Phi Delta Kappa/Gallup poll of the public's attitude toward the public schools. *Phi Delta Kappan*, 77(1), 41–56.

Elam, S.M., Rose, L.C. & Gallup, A.M. (1991). The 23rd annual Phi Delta Kappa/Gallup poll of the public's attitude toward the public schools. *Phi Delta Kappan*, 73(1), 41–56.

Elam, S.M., Rose, L.C. & Gallup, A.M. (1992). The 24th annual Phi Delta Kappa/Gallup poll of the public's attitude toward the public schools. *Phi Delta Kappan*, 74(1), 41–53.

Elam, S.M., Rose, L.C. & Gallup, A.M. (1994). The 26th annual Phi Delta Kappa/Gallup poll of the public's attitude toward the public schools. *Phi Delta Kappan*, 76(1), 41–56.

Elam, S.M., Rose, L.C. & Gallup, A.M. (1996). The 28th annual Phi Delta Kappa/Gallup poll of the public's attitude toward the public schools. *Phi Delta Kappan*, 78(1), 41–59.

Frahm, R. & Covington, J. (1979). *What's happening in minimum competency testing*. Bloomington IN, Phi Delta Kappa. ERIC Document No. ED 175 908.

Gallup, G.H. (1970). The 2nd annual Phi Delta Kappa/Gallup poll of the public's attitude toward the public schools. *Phi Delta Kappan*, 52(2), 99–112.

Gallup, G.H. (1971). The 3rd annual Phi Delta Kappa/Gallup poll of the public's attitude toward the public schools. *Phi Delta Kappan*, 53(1), 33–48.

Gallup, G.H. (1975). The 7th annual Phi Delta Kappa/Gallup poll of the public's attitude toward the public schools. *Phi Delta Kappan*, 57(4), 227–241.

Gallup, G.H. (1976). The 8th annual Phi Delta Kappa/Gallup poll of the public's attitude toward the public schools. *Phi Delta Kappan*, 58(2), 187–200.

Gallup, G.H. (1977). The 9th annual Phi Delta Kappa/Gallup poll of the public's attitude toward the public schools. *Phi Delta Kappan*, 59(1), 33–48.

Gallup, G.H. (1978). The 10th annual Phi Delta Kappa/Gallup poll of the public's attitude toward the public schools. *Phi Delta Kappan*, 60(1), 33–45.

Gallup, G.H. (1984). The 16th annual Phi Delta Kappa/Gallup poll of the public's attitude toward the public schools. *Phi Delta Kappan*, 66(1), 23–38.

Gallup, A.M. & Clark, D.L. (1987). The 19th annual Phi Delta Kappa/Gallup poll of the public's attitude toward the public schools. *Phi Delta Kappan*, 69(1), 17–30.

Gamson, D. (2007). Historical perspectives on democratic decision making in education: Paradigms, paradoxes, and promises, in: P. Moss (Ed.) *Evidence and decision making* (pp. 15–45). The 106th yearbook of the National Society for the Study of Education, Part 1. Malden MA, Blackwell.

Haertel, E. H. & Herman, J. L. (2005). A historical perspective on validity arguments for accountability testing, in: J. L. Herman & E. H. Haertel (Eds.) *Uses and misuses of data for educational accountability and improvement* (pp. 1–34). The 104th yearbook of the National Society for the Study of Education, Part 2. Malden MA, Blackwell.

Hambleton, R. K.., Impara, J., Mehrens, W. & Plake, B. (2000, December). *Psychometric review of the Maryland School Performance Assessment Programme (MSPAP)*. Available online at: http://www.abell.org/pubsitems/ed_psychometric_review_1000.pdf (accessed 30 April 2012).

Jennings, J. & Rentner, D.S. (2006). Ten big effects of the No Child Left Behind Act on public schools. *Phi Delta Kappan*, 88, 110–113.

Johnson, J. & Duffett, A. (2003). *Where are we now? 12 things you need to know about public opinion and public schools* (New York, Public Agenda.

Johnson, J., Arumi, M. & Ott, A. (2006). *Is support for standards and testing fading?* Reality Check 2006, Issue 3. Available online at: http://www.publicagenda.org/files/pdf/rc0603.pdf (accessed February, 2012).

Kane, M. T. (2006). Validation, in: R. L. Brennan (Ed.) *Educational measurement* (4th edn., pp. 17–64). Westport CT, Praeger.

Kirst, M. W. (1985, August). *Sustaining state education reform momentum: the linkage between assessment and financial support.* Public Policy Paper No. 85–C3. ERIC Document No. ED 271 886. Stanford, Institute for Research on Education Finance and Governance, School of Education, Stanford University.

Koretz, D., Stecher, B., Klein, S. & McCaffrey, D. (1994). The Vermont Portfolio Assessment Programme: findings and implications. *Educational Measurement: Issues and Practice*, 13(3), 3–16.

Lerner, B.J. (1982). American education: how are we doing? *Public Interest*, 69, 59–82.

Linn, R.L. (1993). Educational assessment: expanded expectations and challenges. *Educational Evaluation and Policy Analysis*, 15, 1–16.

McDonnell, L. M. (2005). Assessment and accountability from the policymaker's perspective, in: J. L. Herman & E. H. Haertel (Eds) *Uses and misuses of data for educational accountability and improvement* (pp. 35–54). The 104th yearbook of the National Society for the Study of Education, Part 2. Malden MA, Blackwell.

National Commission on Excellence in Education (1983). *A nation at risk: the imperative for educational reform.* Washington, US Government Printing Office. Available online at: http://www2.ed.gov/pubs/NatAtRisk/index.html.

National Education Goals Panel (1991). *The National Educational Goals report: building a nation of learners.* (Washington, Author).

No Child Left Behind Act of 2001 (2002). Pub. L. No. 107–110, 115 Stat. 1425.

Office of Technology Assessment (1992, February). *Testing in American schools: asking the right questions.* OTA-SET-519 Washington, US Government Printing Office.

O'Neill, J. (1994). Aiming for new outcomes: the promise and the reality. *Educational Leadership,* 6, 6–10.

Porter, A.C. (1993). School delivery standards. *Educational Researcher,* 22(5), 24–30.

Porter, T.M. (1995). *Trust in numbers: the pursuit of objectivity in science and public life.* Princeton, Princeton University Press.

Porter, A., McMaken, J., Hwang, J. & Yang, R. (2011). Common core standards: the new US intended curriculum. *Educational Researcher,* 40, 103–116.

Ramanathan, A. (2008). Paved with good intentions: the federal role in the oversight and enforcement of the Individuals with Disabilities Education Act (IDEA) and the No Child Left Behind Act (NCLB). *Teachers College Record,* 110, 278–321.

Rose, L.C. & Gallup, A.M. (2000). The 32nd annual Phi Delta Kappa/Gallup poll of the public's attitude toward the public schools. *Phi Delta Kappan,* 82(1), 41–58.

Rose, L.C. & Gallup, A.M. (2001). The 33rd annual Phi Delta Kappa/Gallup poll of the public's attitude toward the public schools. *Phi Delta Kappan,* 83(1), 41–58.

Rose, L.C. & Gallup, A.M. (2002). The 34th annual Phi Delta Kappa/Gallup poll of the public's attitude toward the public schools. *Phi Delta Kappan,* 84(1), 41–56.

Rose, L.C. & Gallup, A.M. (2003). The 35th annual Phi Delta Kappa/Gallup poll of the public's attitude toward the public schools. *Phi Delta Kappan,* 85(1), 41–56.

Rose, L.C. & Gallup, A.M. (2005). The 37th annual Phi Delta Kappa/Gallup poll of the public's attitude toward the public schools. *Phi Delta Kappan,* 87(1), 41–57.

Rose, L.C. & Gallup, A.M. (2007). The 39th annual Phi Delta Kappa/Gallup poll of the public's attitude toward the public schools. *Phi Delta Kappan,* 89(1), 33–48.

Shepard, L.A. & Bleim, C.L. (1995). Parents' thinking about standardized tests and performance assessments. *Educational Researcher,* 24(8), 25–32.

Spagnolo, J. (1997, March). Perspectives on standard setting from a policy maker's point of view. Paper presented at the *Annual Meeting of the American Educational Research Association,* Chicago. ERIC Document No. ED 412 243.

Waters, B. K. (1981, August). *The test score decline: a review and annotated bibliography.* Technical memorandum 81-2, Directorate for Accession Policy, Office of the Secretary of Defense. Available online at: http://www.dtic.mil/dtic/tr/fulltext/u2/a103091.pdf (accessed 30 April 2012).

The public understanding of error in educational assessment

John Gardner

University of Stirling, UK

Evidence from recent research suggests that in the UK the public perception of errors in national examinations is that they are simply mistakes; events that are preventable. This perception predominates over the more sophisticated technical view that errors arise from many sources and create an inevitable variability in assessment outcomes. The public perception also seems to invest assessment grades and marks with the precision and accuracy of scientific measurements; a perception that does not sit easily with the academic and professional understanding that grades and marks are assigned rather than measured. However, growing numbers of successful challenges by students to their examination results present an interesting challenge for examination bodies. Such evidence could point to a number of possible causes. For example, there might be an increasing awareness among students of the uncertainty surrounding the grades assigned to their work; or their confidence in the capacity of such assessments to reflect the true quality of their performance may be decreasing. As the numbers of challenges increase year on year, there is growing consensus among assessment experts that public confidence needs to be strengthened. Clearly this may be achieved in a number of ways, e.g. by reducing the incidence of human errors and system breakdowns or by improving the public understanding of the assessment process. The latter tactic prompts calls for greater openness and transparency in all aspects of assessment design and process. However, such calls rarely touch on one of the most enduring dimensions of the problem: the public's perception of precision and accuracy in educational assessments. This paper argues that this problem partly arises from a misuse of the term 'measurement' in educational assessment and that in addition to openness and transparency, any public understanding strategy should seek to reduce the misconceptions it causes.

Introduction

Interest in the reliability of educational assessment, in determining the extent of a student's learning and achievement, has witnessed significant growth in recent times. It has, of course, been a long term focus for assessment theorists who seek its minimisation, if not its elimination. Yet error in assessment has multiple sources and manifestations, only a proportion of which can be corrected or avoided. For example, sources of error may include factors such as examination design or a student's personal circumstances, such as health or disposition. Error can also occur in the totalling of marks and scores or they may arise in a more complex manner from the variability in the judgements of examiners.

The technical definition of error may be summarised simply as any variation from the mark, score or grade that characterises the student's 'true' capability in the aspect of their performance that is being assessed. 'True' in this context generally means the specific level of performance that the student would theoretically achieve if all extraneous error conditions were to be removed, i.e. those not relating to the student's intellectual capability in the assessment task. Such a technical definition, however, is largely lost in its translation to the public context. Indeed, research commissioned by the UK examinations regulator, the Office of Qualifications and Examinations Regulation, Ofqual, claims that: 'Fundamentally, the word 'error', in the technical sense it is used by Ofqual, is one which the general public does not use or recognise' (Ipsos MORI, 2009, p. 13). Although the research involved a small sample of 72 people, only half of whom were members of the general public,[1] the conclusion rings true when other manifestations of the *vox populi*, such as media reports, are considered in the round. The participants in the study mostly categorised error as arising from either the candidate's bad luck or mistakes made by examination bodies; the latter being unacceptable at all times.

In a similar study, this time with focus groups comprising postgraduate students, employees, employers, teachers and job seekers (74 participants in total, almost all with degree qualifications), Chamberlain (2010) found that in order to garner their views, she had to address the participants' lack of understanding of reliability in assessment. She did this by asking them to read vignettes that set out examples of possible error circumstances. For example:

> Twin brothers were predicted grade B for A-level Chemistry. One of the twins got his grade B, but the other twin was very disappointed that he got a grade D. What kind of things could have gone right for the first brother, and what could have gone wrong for the second brother? (p. 35)

Chamberlain reported that the participants were able to recognise sources of potential human error in this and similar vignettes but often failed to envisage how this might impact on the reliability of assessment outcomes. Given that most of these participants had been exposed to assessment processes up to degree level, their lack of appreciation of the inevitability of error supports the conclusion that the level of awareness of this inevitability is very low in the wider public arena. Indeed, it could be said that the prevailing populist view is to consider error in assessment in its everyday sense; that it is simply a mistake, something that has been carried out incorrectly.

The demand that errors should not happen in test scores or grades, or examiner judgements, is not an unreasonable position for a member of the public who is unaware of the sophisticated reliability and validity arguments that surround educational assessment. However, the question is begged: is enough being done to inform the public? Arguably, public discussion of the uncertainty that surrounds any assessment outcome is missing from the wider discourse that exists outside of the narrow confines of the professional and academic assessment communities. That said, the fact remains that the assessment community's attempts to convey the complexity of assessment error have long been chastened by a media sensationalism that borders on the mischievous. For example, problems that arose from the routine setting of grade boundaries in UK Advanced Level General Certificate of Education (A-Level) examinations in 2002 were greeted with the *Times Educational Supplement*'s headline: 'How they decided to move the goalposts' (TES, 2002a). In keeping with the TES football analogy, the regulators scored an own-goal in the following year:

> ... any level of error has to be unacceptable—even just one candidate getting the wrong grade is entirely unacceptable for both the individual student and the system. (QCA, 2003)

The phrase 'any level of error has to be unacceptable' is clearly playing to the gallery but more importantly, and with more damage, it assists in perpetuating a false sense of all errors being remediable or avoidable. Whilst an assessment error may be 'unacceptable' to aggrieved individuals, the view of the vast majority of educational assessment experts, including the regulatory body above, is that some degree of error is natural and inevitable. Clearly, acceptance of some degree of error does not eschew the aspiration to make as faultless an assessment of performance as possible but the holy grail of perfectly reliable and valid assessment is indisputably not possible. A greater understanding of error in assessment therefore needs to extend more widely into the education community and its public stakeholders—those being assessed and those using the assessments. This public understanding and interpretation requires the solid foundation of a better awareness of the central issues surrounding the concept of error in educational assessment.

A brief history of error

Error has had a long and infamous history in human discourse. For some it all began back in the mists of time with an apple in an idyllic garden setting. That story details the error of 'sin', the original error of all errors, served by an entire branch of Christian theology, namely Hamartiology. Hamartia first appeared in Aristotle's Poetics as a template for the hero in Greek tragedies who makes a decision that has disastrous consequences, despite its good intentions. According to Sherman (1992), the key meaning of Aristotle's Hamartia was unintentional error, trying to achieve one thing but 'missing the mark'; a meaning that is arguably very apt for assessment. For Aristotle the cause and effect dimensions of error were very broad, for example accident, mistake and wrongdoing (Aristotle, 350BCa); taking the view that there is only one way to hit the mark, and many (unintentional) ways to miss it. According to Hursthouse (2006), Aristotle identified 16 ways to err, all of them in the form of straying away from virtue. Such ostensibly social contexts for error, and the judgments they prompt, tend to follow the strictures of prevailing values and norms rather than any specific evaluative regime, and justified or not, humans have this capacity to establish wrongness as a value judgment, often through an emotional analysis uninfluenced by rationality. In educational assessment, however, this subjectivity has been circumvented through adopting something of a conceit. By implying that its outcomes are actually quantitative 'measurements' of learning or performance arranged in scales, educational assessments give the semblance of rational objectivity. The precision possible with today's scientific instrumentation has attuned the public to expecting measurements to be accurate and precise, whether they are staple measures of the physical world, e.g. time and length, or of more complex phenomena such as a student's learning. However, even scientific measurement is vulnerable to errors and indeed error has a long history in science.

Alder (2002), for example, suggests that until early in the 18th century there were some 250,000 different units for weights and measures in France alone. As such, idiosyncrasy and the lack of standards were greater problems than the concept of error when it came to measures. Even within a specific measuring context, and its set of units, there was no widespread appreciation of error. As one mathematician put it at the time: '... in order to diminish the errors arising from the imperfections of instruments, and of the organs of sense, by taking the Mean [sic] of several observations, has not been so generally received but that some persons, of considerable note, have been of the opinion ... that one single observation, taken with due care, was as much to be relied on as the Mean of a great number' (Thomas Simpson to the Royal Society, 1755 cited by Stigler, 1986, p. 90).

The close of the 18th century saw the emergence of new ways to deal with measurement error, focusing initially on the work of Delambre and Méchain. These French astronomers attempted to 'measure the world' and thereby establish the 'metre' as 'one ten-millionth of the distance between the North Pole and the Equator' (Alder, 2002, p. 1). The metre was to be a measure of length to banish all others; to be unambiguously understood, shared and used by all. However, the two scientists remained constrained by a lack of a 'principled distinction' (p. 315) between precision and accuracy. Despite the improvements offered by the then accepted arithmetic mean of repeated observations, aspects of their astronomical data remained problematic until 1805. It was at that time that Legendre's newly invented least squares method for the treatment of measurement errors was emerging as the signal means of reducing error and identifying the best fit for data. The technique was used on Delambre and Méchain's data and following the publication of the *Base du système mètrique décimal* in 1806, measurement in science took a major leap forward. The least squares method has remained fundamental to error treatment up to the present day and has fostered the ever-increasing

precision and accuracy of science, which prompted Popper to describe it as '...
one of the very few human activities—perhaps the only one—in which errors are
systematically criticised and fairly often, in time, corrected' (1972, p. 216).

From the mid-19th century onwards the new discipline of psychology sought to
extend the allure of measurement precision into the assessment of personal traits
and behaviours, building its own success on the cachet of scientific measurement's
new found trustworthiness. Despite serious underlying debates about the concept
of measurement in human behaviour and attributes (see later in the paper), the
profile of psychometric testing, especially cognitive performance and IQ testing,
went from strength to strength throughout most of the 20th century and was
underpinned by classical test theory (CTT). This theory assumes a stable but
unknown 'true' score in the assessed attribute, for example IQ, which is defined as
the mean score the person would achieve if they were tested an infinite number of
times. The difference between the actual score on the test (the observed score)
and the true score is based on the uncertainty that surrounds the accuracy of any
assessment score. This is usually expressed by the random error E in the equation:

$$X = T + E$$

where X is the observed test score and T is the true score.

Various models under the CTT umbrella may be used to derive the value of the
error term from observed scores. All such attempts, however, must ultimately be
evaluated on what the final score, adjusted for error, is considered to mean; that
is, what it purports to measure. One weakness in this approach is that the true
score can only be assumed to be true for the set of items being considered and
cannot generalise to other sets or combinations. The underlying theory therefore
does not allow for a sufficiently robust treatment of errors and more sophisticated
methods are needed. In recent times, these have derived from item response theory (IRT) approaches to item-based analyses of students' performance in tests. It
is not possible in this paper to do justice to this important area but mention must
be made of the most widely known model, the Rasch method (Rasch, 1960). This
approach taps the assertion that the probability of giving a correct answer to a
question item must be related to the person's intellectual ability in the subject
domain of that item. Using the item parameters: difficulty, discriminating power
and the probability of correctly guessing the answer, IRT approaches are widely
considered to reduce some sources of error in the estimates (not measures) of the
level of ability displayed by each test-taker.

Types of error

To greater or lesser extents, errors can cause difficulties in all disciplines and have
been the subject of various approaches to categorising and understanding them.
For example, engineering disciplines offer us an interesting take on the uncertainty
of measurement with the notion of 'tolerances' and 'allowances'. The former is
designed to accommodate unintended errors in a measure, with an object

considered able to satisfy its intended purpose if its measured dimensions fall between specified boundaries. The latter is a deliberate error condition designed to allow for fluctuations in dimensions, again within bounds, that any object may have to accommodate when the object is being used. Such errors or imprecisions are deliberate and acceptable, though strictly speaking their boundaries are generally precisely fixed.

Writing in the context of economics and decision theory, Loomes and Sugden (1982) postulated an interesting perspective on error that serves to demonstrate that even errors with emotional consequences can be factored into complex statistical approaches to economic modelling. In essence, they postulate two states of mind that are possible when the outcome from a decision between two choices of action becomes known, usually but not exclusively in a financial context. Their Regret Theory identifies that a 'regret' error has occurred when a financial decision turns out not to have been the best one that could have been made in the circumstances. 'Rejoicing' is, predictably, the counter condition!

Human error is arguably multi-faceted in various disciplines. For example, writing in a medical context, McCall and Merry (2002, p. 74) adapted Reason's earlier (1990) definition of human error to focus squarely on the process rather than the outcome of an action:

> ... an unintentional failure in the formulation of a plan by which it is intended to achieve a goal, or an unintentional departure of a sequence of mental or physical activities from the sequence planned, except when such departure is due to a chance intervention.

They set out a taxonomy of errors, reminiscent of Anscombe's 'mistake in performance' vs 'mistake in intention' (1957, section 32, p. 56), summarised as:

- *Skill-based Errors* that include 'lapses and slips', for example occurring when an otherwise expert person is distracted while carrying out an automatic or routine activity.
- *Rule-based Errors* that include the incorrect use of a procedure; or the correct use of a procedure that is in itself incorrect for the circumstances.
- *Knowledge-based Errors* that include not having sufficient knowledge to accomplish the task properly or making a wrong judgement on the basis of what is known.

Such a taxonomy is useful in analysing and assisting our understanding of human errors in assessment systems but each context for error introduces its own nuances. For example, there are system-based errors in educational assessment that are born of short length tests, which cannot begin to sample the full domain of a programme of study, and the 'mistake in performance' taxonomy does not readily cover this error in design. The simple answer, to lengthen the test, will increase its reliability but this approach to error amelioration is obviously limited by the practical and reasonable limits of test duration for candidates. Similarly, one might ask how a generalised classification such as McCall and Merry's could accommodate the ironic errors of students who reach correct answers in multiple choice tests for the wrong reasons, or who choose wrong answers for perfectly valid reasons.

Reason (1990) also identified 'active' and 'latent' errors, with assessment parallels in the former to be found in mis-totalling item scores on an examination script. Most examination bodies have robust means for monitoring and controlling these types of errors but they are never completely eradicable. Illustrations of how well constant vigilance and rigour can successfully reduce clerical mistakes are presented later in Tables 2 and 3.

Latent or underlying errors may be defined as being:

> ... removed from the direct control of the operator and include things such as poor design, incorrect installation, faulty maintenance, bad management decisions and poorly structured organizations. (Kohn *et al.*, 2000, p. 55)

Rhoades and Madaus (2003) have documented examples of US and UK cases of latent errors arising from what they termed the 'closed system' (p. 8) of most large-scale testing. They pointed to the possibility of these errors arising from poor system design, decision-making and policy, and argued that their identification requires in-depth and system-wide investigation. On broadly the same theme, Baird and Coxell (2010) probed the complex relationship between political decisions in three assessment systems and the errors that led to large-scale failures in them. Drawing on these examples from Scotland, New Zealand and England, they identified several key areas that fulfil the definition of latent difficulties prompting systemic error and ultimate failure. These include the dangers of having an assessment policy that is still evolving, the lack of clarity in roles and responsibilities relating to it, and the issue of time slippage and its associated rush to implementation; a problem also addressed in some depth by Oates (2008).

So far, various types of error have been considered, distinguished in some cases by their nature and in others by their source. From the perspective of individuals, errors may be committed by them or by someone else to their or others' detriment. Clearly, it is important to identify the agent and mechanism of any error, if effective attempts are to be made to address it, and that pursuit keeps examination bodies and their candidates ever-vigilant. However, as Newton (2005a, p. 438) puts it:

> Tests and examinations can only be expected to function as blunt instruments; assessment results are best thought of as 'estimates' (Harlen, 1994) or even as 'caricatures' (Mislevy, 1993) of attainment.

To paraphrase Newton from the same paper, assessment results cannot be perfectly reliable or perfectly valid or perfectly comparable. That is not necessarily a bad thing; it is a fact of life. The central problem lies in the capacity of the general public to understand and accept the inherent uncertainty in this situation.

Indications of the public perception of errors in assessment

At present there is evidence to suggest that most people, who are not test-takers themselves, may be unconcerned about reliability issues. For example, each year since 2003 Ipsos MORI have carried out surveys of confidence in the UK public examination system (A-Levels and GCSEs). Table 1 shows a selection of the most recent results of these market research-type surveys covering 2010 and 2011. The surveys explored whether the participants felt that students get the result that their performance warrants and the extent to which they have confidence in the accuracy and quality of the assessment processes.

Aside from the major changes in the student data over the two surveys, for which it is not easy to propose explanations, the teachers', parents' and general public data show reasonable consistency. The general public gave the lowest proportions of positive responses in the range 56–67%. These figures show a majority is content but they also suggest that as much as 33–44% of the general public may have a lack of confidence in the accuracy and quality of assessment in the two types of examinations and may have doubts about whether students get the right grades.

He *et al.* (2010) have investigated the attitudes of teachers (n=314), A-Level students (358) and employers (210) towards reliability and unreliability and confirmed substantial variability in the 'understanding of reliability concepts' (p. 3). They concluded that the respondents' attitudes to different types of assessment error were positively and significantly correlated to their knowledge and experience of the examination process, their understanding of factors that can affect performance or introduce uncertainty in scores, and their approaches to trust more generally. Although the sense of these correlations is plausible, the claims should be treated with some caution as the correlation coefficients were very low, explaining less than 5%, 13% and 19% of the variance for the teacher, student and employer samples respectively.

Tables 2 and 3 illustrate another dimension of confidence in examinations, namely the trends in successful challenges made by UK candidates in relation to their GCSE and A-Level examination grades in the years 2003, 2008 and 2011. Two types of enquiries are reported: requests for clerical re-checking and requests for re-marking.

The proportions of enquiries relating to possible clerical errors in grades remained relatively steady at around 0.02% for GCSE candidates over the period 2003–2011 (in Table 2) and falls to a similar value from 0.6% over the same time frame for A-Level (Table 3). The extent of grade changes arising from clerical error corrections in these tables speaks to the level of detected error being very small, i.e. falling from 1:84,000 to 1:129,000 for GCSE and from 1:29,000 to 1: 181,000 for A-Level.

These figures for clerical re-check requests probably do not include all potentially eligible enquiries. For example, there may have been those who accepted what might have been erroneous results for reasons of expediency, e.g. they had

Table 1. Surveys of confidence in UK examinations (GCSE and A Level) (Source: Ipsos MORI, 2011, 2012)

Year	Teachers		Students		Parents		General Public*	
	2011	2010	2011	2010	2011	2010	2011	2010
Advanced Level General Certificate of Education (A-Level)								
Students get the grade their performance deserves (%)	87	80	76	56	66	68	59	56
Confidence in the accuracy and quality of the marking in A-Level papers (%)	73	73	70	58	54	55	N/A**	N/A
General Certificate of Secondary Education (GCSE)								
Most students get the right grade (%)	75	83	N/A	N/A	N/A	N/A	67	64
Confidence in the accuracy and quality of the marking in GCSE papers (%)	62	64	73	64	58	57	N/A	N/A

*The 'General Public' data represent the responses from a combination of students, parents and members of the public.

**This aspect of the data was not available and could not be disaggregated.

Table 2. Results of enquiries into candidate grades in GCSE examinations for England, Wales and Northern Ireland for 2003, 2008 and 2011 (Sources: QCA, 2004; Ofqual, 2009, 2011)

General Certificate of Secondary Education (GCSE)

Year	2003		2008		2011	
No of Subject* Entries	5,766,862		6,268,151		5,824,300	
	N	%	N	%	N	%
Clerical Re-Check Enquiries**	1,098	0.02	1,161	0.02	1,342	0.02
Clerical Re-Check Grade Changes	69	6.28 of enquiries	86	7.40 of enquiries	45	3.35 of enquiries
Re-Mark Enquiries**	38,440	0.67	85,891	1.37	123,184	2.12
Re-Mark Grade Changes	10,173	26.46 of enquiries	15,825	18.41 of enquiries	20,293	16.47 of enquiries

*This table provides the totals for subject entries rather than 'unit' entries (where units are, for example, the papers making up a subject examination) as the indicator of interest is the proportion of grade changes per subject entry. The official data reports for A-Level (2003, 2008 and 2011) and for GCSE (2008 and 2011) also provide the totals for 'unit' entries. These are not simple multiples of the subject entries as subjects may have different numbers of units and there will always be a proportion of students who only take a sub-set of the available units.
**This check, known as a Service 1 check, ensures that every question has been marked and the total number of marks awarded for each script is correct.
***This Service 2 check comes in two forms: Non-priority and Priority, the latter normally being processed in a shorter time-frame if the candidate is seeking a place at a further or higher education establishment based on their grade profile. Both entail the re-assessment of the work by an examiner who is not the original marker and the figures in the table may include downgrading or upgrading of results. The figures do not disaggregate grade changes made as a result of clerical re-checks, which are an automatic part of the Service 2 re-mark.

Table 3. Results of enquiries into candidate grades in GCE A-Level examinations for England, Wales and Northern Ireland for 2003, 2008 and 2011 (Sources: QCA, 2004; Ofqual, 2009, 2011)

Advanced-Level General Certificate of Education (A-Level)

Year	2003		2008		2011	
No of Subject* Entries	1,831,273		2,188,308		2,536,400	
	N	%	N	%	N	%
Clerical Re-Check Enquiries**	1,090	0.06	1,004	0.05	557	0.02
Clerical Re-Check Grade Changes	64	5.87 of enquiries	50	4.98 of enquiries	14	2.51 of enquiries
Re-Mark Enquiries***	53,335	2.91	68,784	3.14	76,431	3.01
Re-Mark Grade Changes	6,385	11.97 of enquiries	6,907	10.04 of enquiries	10,926	14.29 of enquiries

Key as for Table 2

gained entry to university or the employment of their choice anyway. Such putative additions to the 'eligible' total can be reasonably assumed not to extend the numbers substantially and the overall incidence of such enquiries remains acceptably small. Nevertheless, the media remain quick to pounce on any shortcomings (e.g. BBC News, 2008, 2011; TES, 2008). The dismissal of four examiners for mistakes in totting up marks by one examinations board, and its instruction to 78 others to 'improve their performance', indicates that examination bodies are keen to act swiftly to limit reputational damage (*Guardian*, 17 May 2012).

However, the figures are not so re-assuring in the case of errors by examiners, detected primarily by requested re-marks known as Service 2 enquiries. The proportion of re-mark enquiries leading to a grade change fell over the period for GCSEs (26% to 16%) but the proportion of grade changes to total entries increased from 1:567 to 1:287 (Table 2). For A-Level the corresponding trend in the proportion of re-mark enquiries leading to a grade change remained around 12–14%, with the proportion of grade changes to total entries increasing to a lesser extent than in GCSE, i.e. from 1:287 to 1:232 (Table 3). Again it is reasonable to assume that not all eligible enquiries were made; though generally speaking, A-Levels are higher stakes examinations than GCSEs and candidates may be considered more likely to make an enquiry in 'eligible' circumstances. The trend to a higher proportion of grade changes (against total entry) in both examination systems is interesting as it could signal an increased level of challenge by students against a static level of examiner error or it could signal an increased level of examiner error. The posibilities must remain moot until more research is carried out.

Public confidence in UK assessment risks being jaded by a combination of at least three factors: media sensationalism, the exposure of serious avoidable mistakes on the part of examination bodies and the growing numbers of successful challenges. Certainly this latter issue, relating primarily to errors by examiners, is a growing threat to confidence. However, it has been an enduring problem for many decades. Although usually treated more soberly, Dressel's mischievous perception of a grade being: '... an inadequate report of an inaccurate judgment by a biased and variable judge of the extent to which a pupil has attained an undefined level of mastery of an unknown proportion of an indefinite material' (1983, p. 12) highlights the potential problems in examiners' judgments. In the specific context of tests, but generalisable to all forms of educational assessment, Rhoades and Madaus (2003, p. 29) have argued that the many errors documented in their report:

> ... bear strong witness to the unassailable fact that testing, while providing users with useful information, is a fallible technology, one subject to internal and external errors. This fact must always be remembered when using test scores to describe or make decisions about individuals, or groups of students.

Opposs and He (2011) reproduce an example from the USA of this cautionary approach in the form of a student score report from a North Carolina End-of-Grade Test. In this report, the calculated uncertainty around subscale scores and the final grade are represented graphically by error bars around the given score or grade. A belt-and-braces approach is completed by a narrative declaring a degree of unreliability in the results and advising that: '... instructional and placement decisions should not be based solely on these subscale scores' (p. 30). Interestingly, the participants in Chamberlain's (2010) small-scale study did not support the inclusion of any reliability data, though in their case the proposed reference was a reliability coefficient rather than graphical error bars or numerical error ranges.

The lack of certitude around grades fuels another contentious debate about the extent to which candidates' grades are misclassified in national examinations. Current assessment practices have evolved considerably in sophistication and purpose since the first ever school examinations in 1858 (Cambridge Assessment, 2008) and rigorous quality assurance standards for assessment procedures have been adopted by most examination bodies. Ultimately however, and almost unchanging throughout its history, all educational assessment is based on professional, expert judgement about student performance. And in common with all human judgements, those of assessment professionals can be contested on many grounds; not all of which imply that a mistake has been made. More often than not, perhaps, they will represent legitimate differences of opinion between experts within a field of knowledge.

Nevertheless, students do receive different grades to what their previous performance in the subject would have warranted. Until very recently, much of the debate about classification errors had been informed by theoretical modelling with little by way of empirical evidence of the extent of actual misclassification in a candidate population. Yet it is an issue that over time has regularly surfaced in national testing. Please (1971), for example, was calculating 40% misclassification rates for examination candidates as long ago as 1971 and Willmott and Nuttall (1975) were showing empirically that even with high reliability values of 0.90, misclassification at the level of 25% of candidates in national 16+ examinations was possible. More recently, Wiliam (2001) has claimed 30% misclassification in National Curriculum tests in England. In response, Newton (2003) conceded that even an almost perfect reliability coefficient of 0.99 could allow the misclassification of 5% of candidates but he drew a distinction between 'different classification' and 'misclassification'. The former is considered likely to happen when small differences in scores and the lack of precision in a test render it inappropriate to argue conclusively on which side of a grade boundary a candidate's mark falls. In contrast, misclassification related to relatively large score differences is possible but he concluded that much more empirical work was needed to identify the actual extent of it. One such source of evidence was Gardner and Cowan's (2000, 2005) research that showed that as many as 12,000 of the year 2000 cohort of candidates for the Northern Ireland 11+ examination (with a high test reliability of 0.90) were separated by as few as 18 raw marks across five grade boundaries. Using the standard error of measurement, the possible misclassification was shown to span any three adjacent grade boundaries, potentially misclassifying at least 30% of the candidates and more than ample to cause the loss of a much sought after grammar school place.

Such was the lingering media impact of Wiliam's (2001) claims of 30% misclassification in English National Curriculum tests that Newton (2009) returned to the issue with evidence of consistently high reliability coefficients (mostly over 0.80 and many over 0.90) for various tests including reading, spelling, mathematics and science over the period 1996–2007. He again questioned the magnitude of the earlier claims of misclassification, concluding that it was more likely to be an over-estimate and calling for more research to be carried out into the issue. Several researchers (e.g. Wheadon & Stockford, 2010; Bramley & Dhawan, 2011; Johnston & Johnston, 2011) took up the challenge and Ofqual also devoted a major programme of expert seminars to the debate around reliability. The primary gain from all of this recent work has been a growing consensus on a reduced but still significant theoretical level of 10–15% potential misclassification in candidate populations for National Curriculum tests in mathematics, science and English (see He *et al.*, 2010). However, there remains considerable nervousness around how the complexity of misclassification should be handled, particularly in view of media treatments of such complex issues. Reporting classification accuracy indices as low as 45% (derived from analyses of the performance of GCSE and A-Level test units in the 2008/9 sittings), Wheadon and Stockford (2010) urged caution: 'Until we fully understand them ourselves it would seem dangerous to release them to an unprepared public' (p. 35).

Two points are worthy of note in summarising misclassification errors. The first is that theoretically and practically they cannot be eliminated. The second is that although many factors can cause misclassification there are ways to secure better dependability without loss of rigour. For example, Stanley (2009) has argued that his experience of a state system in Australia, in which 140,000 candidates were annually assessed in high-stakes external examinations and school-based assessments, showed very little evidence of complaint about misclassification. He explained this as being in large measure due to the design of the system, in which the external examination results fell within the range expected on the basis of the prior school-based assessments. Any assessment errors that did occur did not result in significant deviations from expected outcomes.

Tables 2 and 3 showed how problems relating to examiner error in UK examinations can create misclassification errors at a relatively serious level in the grading of student scripts. These human errors can be significantly curtailed through standard quality assurance processes such as examiner training, moderation, double marking and so on. The balance of costs versus perceived benefits is often the arbiter of the extent to which these facilities are employed. However, when the discourse moves from errors in human judgement to the much more fundamental concept of measurement error, the uncertainty around grades can be much more intractable.

The problem of measurement in educational assessment

Measurement is at the heart of assessment error and is arguably a term that is used too loosely in assessment circles. We talk of measuring reasoning ability, measuring competence in this or that skill, and measuring knowledge of this or that subject content. The problem is not simply a case of the wrong use of the word; it is a much more complex web of epistemological positions and their consequences. As mentioned above, the perception that a student's learning or achievement is being assessed by a 'measuring' process prompts many to accept its outcomes as having the same definitive qualities as measurements in more familiar contexts, e.g. length or time. It should come as no surprise then that there has been a long line of scientists prepared to challenge the notion of measurement in psychological or behavioural sciences (for a comprehensive treatment of the topic, see Michell (1999)).

Medawar (1977) was one of the first to broach the issue in public circles. Writing in the *New York Review of Books* (1977, p. 13) he castigated the 'illusion embodied in the ambition to attach a single number valuation to complex quantities'. The field of study he was attacking was IQ and he remarked that 'measurement and numeration' were examples of Gombrich's *idola quantitatis* (the 'idols of quantity').[2] Medawar's polemic, and others like it on the nature of measurement in psychology, reverberates throughout the long history of attempts to assess, in indisputable quantitative terms, students' intellectual abilities and knowledge. Michell (1999) is typical of those scholars who see such a pursuit of measures in psychological research as '... a particularly pernicious form of Pythagoreanism, according to which the ostensibly qualitative features of human life are squeezed insensitively, and without second thought, into a quantitative mould' (p. xiv).

The reference to followers of Pythagoras draws on the Aristotelian critique that 'they construct the whole universe out of numbers' (Aristotle, 350BCb) and is used by Michell as part of his withering analysis of the quantitative dependence that characterised the growth of 'psychophysics' in the second half of the 19th century. He argues that today's widespread misuse, as he sees it, of the term 'measurement' was originally nurtured in the headlong rush to bring the measurement precision of the physical sciences to bear on personal characteristics and behaviour. Much debate centred then and onwards into the 20th century on whether psychological assessments could be legitimately described as measurements. The defining moment was reached when Stevens (1946) declared that 'we may say that measurement, in the broadest sense, is defined as the assignment of numerals to objects and events according to rules' (Stevens, 1946, p. 677). This paper went on to define the operational rules for the nominal, ordinal, interval and ratio scales, now familiar to generations of psychologists as 'measurement' scales. However, Stevens's underlying rationale of assignment rather than measurement has largely been lost and the legacy is the strongly entrenched misconception that educational assessments are actually measures in a scientific sense.

Strictly speaking, a measure in physical science is the ratio relationship between an object's attribute and a unit of magnitude of that attribute. As Michell (1999) explained in the case of a room that is measured as four metres long, it is not the room or its length that is related to the number four, it is the ratio of the attribute of the room being assessed (the length) to the unit of magnitude of length (the metre) that is the number four. The ratio relationship between the length and the unit of magnitude of length (the metre) is four. The number four is therefore not of itself a measure.

As there is no such concept as a standard measure of knowledge, performance in a particular field of study cannot be described by a ratio relationship between the knowledge displayed and any conceivable unit of magnitude of that knowledge. On this basis, arriving at a numerical mark or letter grade for someone's performance in an assessment is certainly not a process of measuring it; it is a process of assigning an appropriate value judgement to it. For example, an assessor who awards a 67% score or a B grade to an essay or portfolio will have done so on the basis of a multi-factorial set of published criteria relating to its content and structure. Depending on subjective differences in the interpretation or emphasis they place on these criteria, different assessors could agree with this assessment, or they could disagree and award different marks, e.g. 73% or 61%, or an A or a C grade. The score or grade is therefore not an accurate and precise measurement; it is an assigned value which may be subject to variability between assessors and does not easily map into a definitive amount of knowledge or understanding. Inter-assessor reliability is an important source of error and Baird and Mac's (1999) meta-analyses of reliability studies from the 1980s demonstrated that even a near perfect reliability estimate of 0.98 may be associated with up to 15% of candidates not achieving the same grade for the same script between examiners. At 0.90 the figures increased to between 40 and 50% not receiving the same grade.

At the more objective, multiple-choice end of the assessment spectrum, the pass mark of 75% in the navigation test for prospective UK pilots[3] unambiguously reflects the minimum number of correct answers a successful candidate must give. However, in terms of the extent of knowledge it reflects, it is not substantially different from a failing score of 74%. It also cannot be assumed to be a measure, in its precise sense, of the knowledge assessed by that test because 75% can be achieved by correctly answering different sets of items within the test. Successful candidates with the same score therefore cannot be assumed to have exactly the same knowledge, or indeed the same lack of knowledge as constituted by the missed 25%. And, of course, even a 100% score would still only reflect that part of the domain of navigation knowledge that has been tested by the questions provided.

Such subtleties of interpretation of test results are rarely exposed or discussed in the public arena. Instead, the use of the term 'measurement' generates unrealistic expectations of the scientific certitude of grades and marks. The consequences are that many people consciously or unconsciously expect that educational assessments should be true representations of a student's learning and performance, consistent from one assessment occasion to another, comparable across assessment contexts (e.g. different subjects and different ways of assessing the same learning) and comparable between students (e.g. 65% for student X should provide the same information about the extent and content of learning as 65% for student Y).

In contrast to the popular notions or expectations, the distinction between 'measurement' and 'assignment' is well understood in the assessment community. For example, the noted Rasch modelling expert, David Andrich, states the problem clearly:

> In education and the social sciences, measurements are used in a way which approximates the use of measurements in the physical sciences. However, the unit and the origin of most assessments are unique to those assessments—there is no natural origin of zero knowledge for example, and no well defined unit such as a pound or a kilogram for mass for measuring the amount of knowledge in any course. ... measurement in education and the social sciences has even more arbitrariness and certainly less conventional agreement on the unit and origin of scale ... the irony is that there is a tendency for greater belief in the consistency of origin and unit in social measurement than there is in physical measurement where their arbitrariness is made explicit. (Andrich, 2005, p. 12)

Recognising that unwarranted interpretations of marks, scores and grades represent one of the major problems in assessment today, Andrich has called for professional development to be provided '... to principals, teachers and students regarding the arbitrariness of measurement units in educational assessment' (p. 13).

Concluding remarks

Error in educational assessment comes in many guises but central to all of them is that the outcome of the assessment is not as it should be; someone or something is at fault. It would be rare for error to be generated deliberately, so for the most part it can be assumed to be unintentional. It may be the fault of humans, machines or systems. It may be random or systematic, latent or active. It may arise from poor judgement, inadequate information or inappropriate procedures. It may be the result of individual student circumstances and dispositions.

With so many sources, so many types and so many contexts for error, logic and experience lead us to a simple conclusion. Error cannot be entirely eradicated. Educational assessment, therefore, should always be considered to be a probabilistic process and the task for the assessment community is to promote the reality that all educational assessments are approximate.

The keys to making the probabilistic foundations of assessment part and parcel of everyday understanding lie in openness and transparency in assessment design, process and reporting. Standards for transparency and reporting of assessment have existed in detailed form in the USA since 1985 (AERA, APA and NCME, 1999) and have been adopted widely around the world but curiously not in the UK; though a variety of researchers (e.g. Gardner & Cowan, 2000, 2005; Newton 2005b, 2009) have periodically called for UK examination bodies to use them. However, the most recent report from Ofqual on reliability in assessment (Opposs

& He, 2011) is unequivocal in setting out a series of recommendations for UK assessment that broadly reflects what is already in these internationally accepted standards. It also calls for a long-term strategy to improve public understanding through, for example, providing the media with better explanations of technical terms and processes, the use of plain language and better support for interpretation.

In part at least, all such calls are being made because there is a perception that trust in the examination system is being eroded, particularly by the media's often sensationalist treatment of error-related problems. However, there is also a growing recognition that if presented consistently and in an appropriate manner, the general public will better understand the complexity and variability surrounding educational assessment. This paper therefore argues the need to recognise the unintentional conceit of implied accuracy and precision, which is involved in using the term 'measurement' to describe a process of 'assigning' grades or marks. As part of any attempt to improve the public understanding of assessment, the assessment community should strive to make it clear that measurement in the scientific sense is not what we do in educational assessment.

Acknowledgement

I very much appreciated the comments of Hugh Morrison, Paul Black and Gordon Stanley on earlier drafts of this paper. However, responsibility for the positions I have taken rests entirely with me.

Notes

1. The research involved two sets of focus group interviews and the other 36 participants comprised teachers, students and examiners.
2. Ernst Gombrich later developed (1979) his idols vs ideals argument in a series of essays on values in the humanities, in which he criticised the seeming imperative to collect and analyse numerical data for every scholarly pursuit.
3. Civil Aviation Authority's pass-mark for the Joint Aviation Regulations-Flight Crew Licensing (JAR-FCL) Theoretical Knowledge Examinations, see http://www.caa.co.uk/docs/175/srg_lts_LASORS2010_Section%20J.pdf

References

AERA, APA and NCME (1999). *Standards for educational and psychological testing American Educational Research Association, American Psychological Association and National Council for Mathematics Education.* Washington, DC, American Psychological Association.

Alder, K. (2002). *The measure of all things.* London, Abacus.

Andrich, D. (2005). *A report to the Curriculum Council of Western Australia regarding assessment for tertiary selection.* Available online at: http://www.curriculum.wa.edu.au/internet/Communications/Publications.

Anscombe, G.E.M. (1957). *Intention* (2nd edn.). Cambridge, Harvard University Press. Available online at: http://www.scribd.com/doc/8263181/Intention-second-edition-GEM-Anscombe.

Aristotle (c. 350 BCa). *Nicomachean ethics Bk II.6.* Adelaide, University of Adelaide. Available online at: http://ebooks.adelaide.edu.au/a/aristotle/nicomachean/

Aristotle (c. 350 BCb). *Metaphysics Bk XIII.6.* Adelaide, University of Adelaide. Available online at: http://ebooks.adelaide.edu.au/a/aristotle/metaphysics/complete.html.

Baird, J-A. & Coxell, A. (2010). *Policy, latent error and systemic examination failures.* Association for Educational Assessment—Europe, CADMO (in press).

Baird, J. & Mac, Q. (1999). How should examiner adjustments be calculated? A discussion paper. *AEB Research, Report,* RC13.

BBC (2008, 17 July). More questions about Sats results. Available online at: http://news.bbc.co.uk/1/hi/education/7511922.stm.

BBC (2011, 9 June). Students hit by more exam errors. Available online at: http://www.bbc.co.uk/news/education-13710868.

Bramley, T. & Dhawan, V. (2011). *Estimates of reliability of qualifications.* Coventry, Office of Qualifications and Examinations Regulation. Available online at: http://www.ofqual.gov.uk/index.php?option=com_content&view=article&id=768

Cambridge Assessment (2008). *How have school exams changed over the past 150 years?* Available online at: http://www.cambridgeassessment.org.uk/ca/News_Room/Latest_News/News?id=124622

Chamberlain, S. (2010). *Public perceptions of reliability.* Coventry, Office of Qualifications and Examinations Regulation. Available online at: http://www.ofqual.gov.uk/files/Ofqual_10_4708_public_perceptions_reliability_report_08_03_10.pdf

Dressel, P. (1983). Grades: one more tilt at the windmill, in: A.W. Chickering (Ed.) *Bulletin.* Memphis, Memphis State University.

Gardner, J. & Cowan, P. (2000). *Testing the test: a study of the reliability and validity of the Northern Ireland Transfer Procedure Test in enabling the selection of pupils for grammar school places.* Belfast, Queen's University Belfast. Available online at: http://arrts.gtcni.org.uk/gtcni/bitstream/2428/6312/1/Testing%20the%20Test.pdf

Gardner, J. & Cowan, P. (2005). The fallibility of high stakes '11-plus' testing in Northern Ireland. *Assessment in Education: Principles, Policy and Practice,* 12(2), 145–165.

Gombrich, E.H. (1979). *Ideals and idols: essays on values in history and in art.* Oxford, Phaidon.

Guardian (2012, 17 May). Examiners axed after marking mistakes. Available online at: http://www.guardian.co.uk/education/2012/may/17/examiners-axed-after-marking-mistakes

Harlen, W. (1994). Developing public understanding of education—a role for researchers. *British Educational Research Journal,* 20(1), 3–16.

He, Q., Hayes, M. & Wiliam, D. (2010). Classification accuracy in results from key stage 2 National Curriculum tests, in: *The reliability compendium.* Coventry, Office of Qualifications and Examinations Regulation. Available online at: http://www.ofqual.gov.uk/standards/reliability/

He, Q., Opposs, D. & Boyle, A. (2010). *A quantitative investigation into public perceptions of reliability in examination results in England.* Coventry, Office of Qualifications and Examinations Regulation. Available online at: http://www.ofqual.gov.uk/index.php?option=com_content&view=article&id=780

Hursthouse, R. (2006). The central doctrine of the mean, in: R. Kraut (Ed.) *The Blackwell guide to Nicomachean Ethics*. Oxford, Blackwell.

Ipsos MORI (2009). *Public perceptions of reliability in examinations: a research study conducted for Ofqual*. Coventry, Office of Qualifications and Examinations Regulation. Available online at: http://www.ofqual.gov.uk/2320.aspx

Ipsos MORI (2011). *Perceptions of A-Levels and GCSE—Wave 9*. Coventry, Office of Qualifications and Examinations Regulation. Available online at: http://www.ofqual.gov.uk/files/2011-03-perceptions-of-a-levels-and-gcse-wave-9.pdf

Ipsos MORI (2012). *Perceptions of A-Levels, GCSE and other qualifications—Wave 10*. Coventry, Office of Qualifications and Examinations Regulation. Available online at: http://www.ofqual.gov.uk/files/2012-03-13-ofqual-perceptions-of-a-levels-gcses-wave-10.pdf

Johnston, S. & Johnston, R. (2011). *Component reliability in GCSE and GCE*. Coventry, Ofqual 11/4780. Available online at: http://www2.ofqual.gov.uk/index.php?option=com_content&view=article&id=767

Kohn, L.T., Corrigan, J.M. & Donaldson, M.S. (2000). *To err is human: building a safer health system*. Washington, DC, Institute of Medicine, National Academies Press.

Loomes, G. & Sugden, R. (1982). Regret Theory: an alternative theory of rational choice under uncertainty. *The Economic Journal*, 92(368), 805–824.

McCall-Smith, A. & Merry, A. (2002). *Errors, medicine and the law*. New York, Cambridge University Press.

Medawar, P. B. (1977, 3 February). Unnatural science. *The New York Review of Books*.

Michell, J. (1999). *Measurement in psychology: a critical history of a methodological concept*. Cambridge, Cambridge University Press.

Mislevy, R.J. (1993). Foundations of a new test theory, in: N. Frederiksen, R.J. Mislevy & I.I. Bejar (Eds) *Test theory for a new generation*. New Jersey, Lawrence Erlbaum Associates.

Newton, P. (2003). The defensibility of national curriculum assessment in England. *Research Papers in Education*, 18(2), 101–127.

Newton, P.E. (2005a). The public understanding of measurement inaccuracy. *British Educational Research Journal*, 31(4), 419–442.

Newton, P.E. (2005b). Threats to professional understanding of assessment error. *Journal of Education Policy*, 20, 457–483.

Newton, P.E. (2009). The reliability of results from national curriculum testing in England. *Educational Research*, 51(2), 181–212.

Oates, T. (2008). Going round in circles: temporal discontinuity as a gross impediment to effective innovation in education and training. *Cambridge Journal of Education*, 38(1), 105–120.

Ofqual (2009). *Enquiries about appeals and results: report on the summer 2008 GCSE and A-Level examinations series*, Ofqual/09/4126. Coventry, Office of Qualifications and Examinations Regulation. Available online at: http://www.ofqual.gov.uk/files/2009-03-18-ear-appeals.pdf

Ofqual (2011). *Enquiries about appeals and results: report on the summer 2011 GCSE and A-Level examinations series*, Ofqual/11/5016. Coventry, Office of Qualifications and Examinations Regulation. Available online at: http://www.ofqual.gov.uk/files/2011-12-07-enquiries-about-results-2011.pdf

Opposs, D. & He, Q. (2011). *The reliability programme: final report*. Coventry, Office of the Qualifications and Examinations Regulator. Available online at: http://www.ofqual.gov.uk/files/reliability/11-03-16-Ofqual-The-Final-Report.pdf.

Please, N.W. (1971). Estimation of the proportion of examination candidates who are wrongly graded. *British Journal of Mathematics, Statistics and Psychology*, 24(2), 230–238.

Popper, K. (1972). *Conjectures and refutations* (4th edn.). London, Routledge & Kegan Paul (statement actually made in 1963).

QCA (2003). *A Level of preparation*. Qualifications and Curriculum Authority insert in the Times Educational Supplement, 4 April.

QCA (2004) (updated 2005). *Enquiries about appeals and results: report on the summer 2003 GCSE and A-Level examinations series.* Coventry, Office of Qualifications and Examinations Regulation. Available online at: http://dera.ioe.ac.uk/14586/1/QCA_05_1608_2004_published_report_17_5_051.pdf

Rasch, G. (1960). *Probabilistic models for some intelligence and attainment tests.* Copenhagen, Danish Institute for Educational Research.

Reason, J. (1990). *Human error.* Cambridge, Cambridge University Press.

Rhoades, K. & Madaus, G. (2003). *Errors in standardized tests: a systemic problem.* Boston, MA, Boston College/National Board on Educational Testing and Public Policy.

Sherman, N. (1992). *Hamartia* and virtue, in: A.O. Rorty (Ed.) *Essays on Aristotle's Poetics.* Princeton, NJ, Princeton University Press.

Stanley, G. (2009). Reliability: a practitioner's perspective. Paper presented at *Ofqual Launch of Chief Regulator's Report*, 7 May. Office of Qualifications and Examinations Regulation. Available online at: http://www.ofqual.gov.uk/files/2009-05-07-reliability-speech-gordon-stanley.pdf

Stevens, S.S. (1946). On the theory of scales of measurement. *Science, New Series*, 103(2684), 677–680.

Stigler, S.M. (1986). *The history of statistics.* Massachusetts, Belknap Harvard.

TES (2002, 27 September). How they decided to move the goalposts. Available online at: http://www.tes.co.uk/article.aspx?storycode=369055

TES (2008, 11 July). Examiners allowed eight times the mistakes. Available online at: http://www.tes.co.uk/article.aspx?storycode=2646953

Wheadon, C. & Stockford, I. (2010). Classification accuracy and consistency in GCSE and A-Level examinations offered by the Assessment and Qualifications Alliance (AQA) November 2008 to June 2009, in: Ofqual (2011). *The reliability compendium.* Coventry, Office of Qualifications and Examinations Regulation. Available online at: http://www.ofqual.gov.uk/standards/reliability/

Wiliam, D. (2001). Reliability, validity and all that jazz. *Education 3–13*, 29(3), 17–21.

Willmott, A.S. & Nuttall, D.L. (1975). *The reliability of examinations at 16+.* London, Macmillan Education.

Ofqual's Reliability Programme: a case study exploring the potential to improve public understanding and confidence

Paul E. Newton

Cambridge Assessment, UK

In May 2008, Ofqual established a two-year programme of research to investigate the nature and extent of (un)reliability within the qualifications, examinations and assessments that it regulated. It was particularly concerned to improve understanding of, and confidence in, this technically complex and politically sensitive phenomenon. The following article presents an account of this programme, from the perspective of one of its initiators, the author. It describes: the context prior to the programme, where little information on (un)reliability was routinely available to the public; the rationale for the programme, in terms of the tension between improving public understanding and the concomitant threat of decreasing public confidence; and ways in which aspects of the programme were constructed through media reports. It concludes with lessons learned from running the programme and with an extended discussion of the challenge of talking about reliability and error.

Secondary school examining in England

There is a long history of external examining at the end of secondary schooling in England, both at age 16 ('school leaving examinations') and at age 18 ('university entrance examinations'). The system that exists today has its roots in Local Examinations which were established by the universities of Oxford and Cambridge in 1857 and 1858, respectively (Roach, 1971). It became a truly national system in 1918, with the advent of School Certificate and Higher School Certificate examinations, which seven university bodies were approved to offer (Petch, 1953). To help regulate this system, the Secondary School Examinations Council was established to oversee comparability of standards across the examining bodies.

Over the years, the examination system has evolved, but has not changed radically. School leaving and university entrance examinations are still awarded by a range of organisations, many of which have their roots in the seven university bodies. Students are still examined in a fairly wide range of subjects at age 16, and in a fairly narrow range of subjects at age 18. The examinations are still heavily based upon the constructed response format, which means that the system is still heavily reliant upon external examiners, typically practising teachers, who are appointed by the examining boards each year to mark scripts.

The regulatory structure has been tightened substantially in recent years, with the establishment of Ofqual, which regulates qualifications offered in England. Five examining boards offer school examinations in England, both for the General Certificate of Secondary Education (GCSE) and for the General Certificate of Education Advanced level (A-level). These examinations are offered in a wide range of subjects, offering students an element of choice at GCSE and a substantial amount of choice at A-level. Although almost all of the national cohort takes GCSEs in English and mathematics (in the order of around 600,000 students), numbers taking some of the more obscure GCSEs and A-levels may be no greater than a few hundred. Further insights into the history and nature of examining in England can be found in Tattersall (2007) and Newton (2007).

Despite the longevity of the system, it has not always been held in high respect, and has come in for criticism repeatedly over the years. Procedures for marking and grading examinations have been a particular focus for public debate. Early on, the system survived a major onslaught on the written examination format, mounted by prominent academics (see Hartog & Rhodes, 1935; Lawn, 2008). Yet concerns over marking accuracy are a constant refrain, even to the present day.

Since at least the 1970s, national pass-rates have been the subject of constant debate, for both school leaving and university entrance examinations. In the 1970s and 1980s, the general public was sceptical of stable pass-rates; today, it is sceptical of rising pass-rates (see Newton, 2011). Although, in recent years, procedures operated by the examining boards have become more transparent than ever before, there is a still a lack of public awareness of the technical detail of examining, which can be quite complex and arcane. The situation is not as bad as it was in the 1960s, however, when one prominent academic described the work of the boards as shrouded in a 'cloak of secrecy' (Wiseman, 1961). Having said that, even the regulatory authorities have come in for criticism, in recent years, for their reticence to publish uncomfortable research (see Mansell, 2003).

Public understanding vs. public confidence

Ofqual was launched, during May 2008, as the Office of the Qualifications and Examinations Regulator. It was technically still the regulatory arm of its parent organisation, the Qualifications and Curriculum Authority (QCA), although its re-branding pointed towards an entirely independent role that would require a change in primary legislation. Although, in law, it only became an independent entity on 1 April 2010, in practice, it operated fairly independently of QCA from its launch.

In the wake of the Apprenticeship, Skills, Children and Learning Act, of 2009, Ofqual became known as the Office of Qualifications and Examinations Regulation. The Act established five objectives for Ofqual, of which three are particularly significant to the present discussion:

- qualifications standards objective—to secure the reliability of qualifications
- public confidence objective—to promote public confidence in qualifications
- awareness objective—to promote awareness and understanding of qualifications.

These objectives crystallised a dilemma. The qualifications standards objective obliged the regulator to ensure that evidence of qualification reliability was produced, without which its success in achieving the objective could not be monitored. Indeed, as implied by the awareness objective, the evidence would need to be made public; not simply for accountability purposes, but also to improve public understanding. However, since there is no such thing as perfectly reliable assessment, evidence of reliability is simultaneously evidence of unreliability. Since the publication of evidence of unreliability has the potential to threaten public confidence, pursuit of the qualifications standards objective had the potential to threaten achievement of the public confidence objective.

This quandary was explored, from first principles, in Newton (2005a). While the risks of improving public understanding of reliability and error were acknowledged, it was argued that the risks associated with not improving public understanding were greater. In an age of increasing accountability, evidence of error is increasingly likely to reach the attention of the public. It was hypothesised that the impact of this information would differ according to the manner in which it became public. If it were to become public as the result of a carefully managed campaign to improve public understanding, then this would minimise the threat to public confidence. If it were to become public as the result of whistle-blowing from internal informers, or from the publication of damning research by external researchers (e.g. Hartog & Rhodes, 1935), then this would maximise the threat to public confidence.

During the May 2008 launch event, the (then) new Chair of Ofqual announced a two-year programme of research and analysis to investigate reliability:

> As the regulator of qualifications in England I believe that it is essential for all of us to understand better the reliability of assessments in our national systems [...]. I can, therefore, tell you today that Ofqual will undertake an in-depth programme of work—call it a health check—on the reliability of tests, examinations and teacher assessments, in this country. (Tattersall, 2008)

The Reliability Programme constituted a case study through which to explore the promotion of public understanding of reliability and error. It would provide evidence concerning the consequences of greater openness and transparency about educational measurement inaccuracy—in the context of a carefully managed campaign to improve public understanding—and would provide insights into the success, or otherwise, of strategies used to achieve this end.

As Head of Assessment Research at Ofqual, I contributed to the establishment of this programme and supported its roll-out until the middle of 2009 when I took up a position at Cambridge Assessment. Final programme reports were published early in 2011 (Baird *et al.*, 2011; Burslem, 2011; Opposs & He, 2011). Having monitored the impact of the programme throughout its duration, in terms of how it was being represented through media reporting, I was in a position to produce the following analysis by the end of 2011.

The following account is focused upon the representation of the programme, the representation of its agents, and the representation of reliability and error, through media reporting, specifically newspaper reports. Although Ofqual publishes information on its website, and makes presentations at seminars and conferences, media reporting is still fundamental to ensuring a wide audience. In the absence of media reporting, the outcomes of any programme would be unlikely ever to impact upon either public understanding or public confidence. The study of media reporting can therefore provide important insights into the potential for influencing public understanding and confidence (e.g. Warmington & Murphy, 2004; Newton, 2005b). Although these insights are important, they are only part of the story, of course, since media reports do not provide direct evidence of either public understanding or confidence. They provide evidence of the construction of a narrative that is deemed, by media editors, to be worthy of public attention, thereby providing a filter for public understanding and confidence.

As an interpretive account, the following discussion is necessarily subjective, and it should be read with the understanding that it was written from the perspective of someone who believed in the importance of enhancing public confidence in qualifications through improving public understanding of reliability and error.

Reporting reliability research

From a technical perspective, reliability concerns the consistency of an assessment procedure, i.e. the likelihood that a student would end up with the same mark or grade were the assessment to be replicated. Although generic assessment procedures stay the same from one replication to the next, all sorts of minor circumstantial things do change (e.g. different questions, different markers), any of which might lead to a different assessment outcome. Causes of unreliability can be classified as:

- occasion-related (e.g. if assessed on another day, the student might have been less tired)

- test-related (e.g. if a different test had been set, the student might not have been disadvantaged by the unfamiliar wording of one essay title or advantaged by the topic of another)
- marking-related (e.g. if a different marker had been assigned, the student might have been marked down for using unusual stylistic constructions), and
- grading-related (e.g. if a different team of people had been involved in the process of grading, different cut-scores might have been set).

The unreliability of public examination results has been recognised, and theorised, for well over a century (e.g. Edgeworth, 1888). Over the years, the examining boards have gone to great lengths to minimise threats to reliability; ranging from the development of extensive qualification and training procedures for examiners, to fundamental research into factors that influence consistent marking (e.g. Greatorex & Bell, 2004; Crisp & Johnson, 2007; Crisp, 2008; Suto & Greatorex, 2008a, b; Black *et al.*, 2011). Despite this, prior to the outset of the Reliability Programme, there was only limited published research into *levels* of reliability that can be expected of public examinations in England (e.g. Murphy, 1978; Newton, 1996). This stood in stark contrast to a wealth of research into the comparability of public examinations, a topic that had dominated public debate since the introduction of the national system of examining in 1918. Part of the intention of the Reliability Programme was therefore to redress this imbalance.

The context prior to the programme

The context immediately prior to the commencement of the Reliability Programme was one of growing concern over the reliability of results from national assessments. As documented in a Joint Memorandum to the Select Committee inquiry into *Testing and Assessment*, Paul Black, John Gardner & Dylan Wiliam (2007) asked:

IS ENOUGH KNOWN ABOUT ERROR IN OUR PUBLIC EXAMINATIONS?

> The short answer to this question is 'no'. One of us (PJB) wrote to the chief executive of the QCA, in January 2005, enquiring whether there were any well researched results concerning the reliability of those tests for which the QCA had responsibility. The reply was that 'there is little research into this aspect of the examining process', and drew attention only to the use of borderline reviews and to the reviews arising from the appeals system. (Black *et al.*, 2007)

These academics were not simply worried about the lack of published evidence, they were concerned that reliability might actually be very low and that this was being covered up. A few years earlier, Wiliam (2001) had published estimates from a rough simulation that had led him to believe that National Curriculum test results were incorrect for around 30% of students. Despite bringing this analysis to the attention of the QCA, evidence to the contrary was not forthcoming. The

Select Committee inquiry provided an opportunity to interrogate the QCA Chief Executive, Ken Boston, and he responded as follows:

> Error exists. As I said before, this is a process of judgment. Error exists, and error needs to be identified and rectified where it occurs. I am surprised at the figure of 30%. We have been looking at the range of tests and examinations for some time. We think that is a very high figure, but whatever it is it needs to be capable of being identified and corrected. (HCCSFC, 2008)

The Select Committee also interrogated senior civil servants, including Jon Coles, who responded as follows:

> Annette Brooke: I did ask the Qualifications and Curriculum Authority what it was doing to investigate the matter. I was not very satisfied that it was checking out the figure. I think that it is important to check it out. Perhaps you could ask them to do it, and then you can put your hands up and say that there is not a 30% error rate.

> Jon Coles: I can say that without asking QCA to do any further work, because QCA regulates the exam system robustly. I can say to you without a shadow of a doubt—I am absolutely convinced—that there is nothing like a 30% error rate in GCSEs and A-levels. If there is some evidence that that is the case, I would really welcome knowing what it is.

> Chairman: Jon, let us agree that together we will get to the bottom of this. (HCCSFC, 2008)

The context immediately prior to the announcement of the programme was therefore very germane to it. There had been no whistle-blowing from internal informers, and the critique from external researchers was more about demanding evidence than furnishing it. In a sense, then, this context invited the regulator to respond with a carefully managed campaign to improve public understanding, or else risk the consequences of not doing so. Responding with a campaign like this would not be easy, of course, since uncovering evidence of unreliability would present a threat to the status quo. The launch of the regulator provided an opportunity for Ofqual to demonstrate its new-found independence in a responsible way, through the establishment of the Reliability Programme, showing its readiness to look with an expert and impartial eye under stones that others might prefer to have left unturned.

The Programme

The Reliability Programme divided into three strands:

(1) Generating evidence on the reliability of results from a selection of national qualifications, examinations and other assessments in England through empirical studies.
(2) Interpreting and communicating evidence on reliability.
(3) Investigating public perceptions of reliability and developing regulatory policy on reliability.

To support this work, two Advisory Groups were formed: a Technical Advisory Group, which supported Strand 1; and a Policy Advisory Group, which supported Strands 2 and 3. The work of the Policy Advisory Group was particularly relevant to the present discussion, with a remit to explore ways to improve public understanding of reliability concepts, communicate reliability evidence to the public and increase public confidence in the examinations system.

A substantial programme of research was commissioned to generate evidence relating to each of the three strands. This involved researchers from general and vocational awarding bodies, researchers operating in an independent capacity, and researchers from the regulator. A compendium of findings was published by Ofqual during summer 2011 (see http://www.ofqual.gov.uk/standards/reliability), and subsequently in hard copy too (Opposs & He, 2012). The hard copy included 22 chapters and ran to over 900 pages.

The programme generated a wealth of new information on levels of reliability associated with national assessments, examinations and qualifications. Some of this challenged conclusions from previous research; for example, evidence was provided that results from National Curriculum tests were not as unreliable as Wiliam (2001) had previously suggested (see also He & Opposs, 2012). The programme also generated important insights into attitudes towards, and understanding of, reliability amongst teachers, students, employers and other members of the public. It revealed substantial variability in both attitudes and understanding, both within and between the different groups. The Policy Advisory Group recommended that examining boards and awarding bodies should be encouraged to continue generating and publishing evidence on reliability, and that a programme should be established to improve public understanding and to increase public confidence. Officially, the Reliability Programme had a two-year life-span, although the intention of the regulatory policy on reliability, stemming from Strand 3, was that it would result in the routine publication of an appropriate body of evidence each year.

Before turning to the discussion of lessons learned from running the programme, in the light of media coverage, a brief word on terminology will illustrate just how complicated the task of improving public understanding can be. Two terms need to be explained: reliability and measurement inaccuracy. As the name suggests, the Reliability Programme was notionally concerned with the former, a narrow technical concept indicating the likelihood that a student would end up with the same mark or grade, were the assessment to be replicated. From this perspective, reliability is only concerned with random, i.e. unsystematic error. However, this is only part of the story, since there is another kind of error, systematic error, that is normally discussed under the banner of validity.

The term measurement inaccuracy is used in the remainder of this paper to indicate a broad conception of error, which embraces both the systematic and unsystematic. From this perspective, whenever the mark or grade that a student ought to have been awarded (given their level of attainment on the day they sat their exam) differs from the mark or grade that they actually were awarded, this can be described as error, in the sense of measurement inaccuracy. This is the sense of error, i.e. result incorrectness, that was typically associated with media reporting of the 30% figure from Wiliam (2001):

> 30 per cent of pupils may be given the wrong test level, a finding which ministers have never disproved. (Mansell, 2006)

From the outset of the programme, therefore, there lurked a major latent challenge to public understanding. While the technical studies within Strand 1 focused tightly upon the narrow technical concept of reliability, this was not necessarily true of the studies within Strands 2 and 3, which were focused on public understanding. Since members of the public are unlikely to draw any sharp distinction between unsystematic and systematic causes of error, and are unlikely ever to need to, the all-encompassing concept of measurement inaccuracy was more apposite. Thus, the studies within Strands 2 and 3 tended to imply a broader conception of error than those within Strand 1.[1]

The construction of the Reliability Programme

The focus of the following discussion is upon lessons learned from running a carefully managed campaign to improve public understanding, as revealed through media constructions. To many within the examining community, the Reliability Programme constituted a major hostage to fortune, risking the very confidence in the system that sustains the currency of examination grades. The following sections consider the extent to which such fears were justified and challenges that were encountered along the way. They illustrate ways in which well-informed and well-intentioned communications can be undermined by subsequent media reporting.

The construction of whistle-blowing

The very act of trying to be more open about the nature and extent of unreliability in public examinations carries a risk: the risk that it is reported not as an attempt to inform or to educate (i.e. to improve public understanding) but as an attempt to undermine or to disrupt (i.e. to reduce public confidence).

The media play a central role in this respect, potentially making this risk a reality through exaggeration, selective reporting or, less frequently, misreporting. The best illustration of this occurred in response to a presentation of mine, delivered to Cambridge Assessment during December 2008 (Newton, 2008a). The presentation was video-recorded and subsequently made publicly available through the Cambridge Assessment website in January 2009.

The seminar made the front page of the *Telegraph* with a strap-line that read: 'Up to a third of schoolchildren may receive the wrong test results, according to the exams regulator' (Paton, 2009a). This was misleading, since I referred to the 30% figure from Wiliam (2001) only to explain why the real figure was likely to be much lower than this. The report then opened:

> The examinations system is so error-ridden that it is 'inevitable' some pupils will get inaccurate grades, it was claimed.
>
> Dr Paul Newton, head of assessment research at Ofqual, which was set up by Gordon Brown to vet standards in national tests, said marking was not completely reliable. (Paton, 2009a)

To an assessment professional, the information contained in these first two sentences reads like a statement of the obvious—some students will always get the wrong grade and marking is not completely reliable. The very fact that it could constitute (front page) news makes it clear how challenging it can be to manage a campaign to improve public understanding. Whether or not any member of the general public has ever actually believed that examination marking is completely reliable, the myth of perfect marking still provided a viable media template from which an ostensibly shocking news story could be constructed. (See Warmington & Murphy, 2004, for an extended discussion of media templates.)

What this illustrates is not that the public are ignorant of marking unreliability. Indeed, research from the Reliability Programme identified that this is not generally true (e.g. He *et al.*, 2011). What it illustrates is that it is still possible for public understanding to be constructed in this manner; and, therefore, when faced with evidence of marking unreliability, that it is still possible for the boards to be constructed as being afraid of the public finding out. This potential for construction presents a subtle challenge. It will inevitably be related to public understanding—if the nature and prevalence of marking error had been better understood, then it might have been harder for the *Telegraph* to have run the above report as though it constituted news—yet how the public understands unreliability and how the public can be constructed as understanding it are different beasts, and need to be tackled in different ways.

Of course, a story about a whistle-blower will always be more sexy than a story about an educator. So the risk of being portrayed as undermining the system will always be high when attempting to improve public understanding of measurement inaccuracy. This was clearly the intention of a report in the *MailOnline*, the following day:

> Dr Paul Newton blew the whistle on the 'inevitable' inaccuracy in the marking of tests taken by hundreds of thousands of children every year. (Ross, 2009)

The fact that the story did not run far beyond these two reports suggests that the inappropriate construction posed a limited threat to system stability, which might either relate to its limited plausibility to members of the public, or to its limited significance. Finally, it is worth emphasising that both of these reports contained a considerable amount of useful coverage of the main points of the presentation; albeit alongside elements of exaggeration, selective reporting and misleading.

The construction of trivialisation

One very effective way to educate is through the use of analogy, e.g. using the analogy of medical misdiagnosis to help people to understand measurement inaccuracy (Newton, 2008b). However, the use of analogy can backfire, as the Chief Executive of Ofqual, Isabel Nisbet, discovered to her cost:

> Ms Nisbet said: 'People don't believe that it is a scandal that there is variability in marking of extended English answers. They understand that that is what you would expect.
>
> 'You just need to watch Strictly Come Dancing to see the variability of some of the judgments of experts. So people do understand that.'
>
> But her views seem at odds with those of Ofqual chair Kathleen Tattersall, who last week said of the QCA research on marking: 'The high level of misclassification in English suggests significant cause for concern.'
>
> Mary Bousted, general secretary of the Association of Teachers and Lecturers, said: 'That is incredibly patronising and naive. The fact that nearly half of pupils appear to have been given the wrong level must be a huge concern to the children, whose school careers could be blighted, to the parents, and to the teachers, whose performance management is increasingly based on the levels pupils achieve.
>
> 'Strictly Come Dancing is good entertainment, but the test levels that pupils achieve affect their lives. To compare the two is demeaning.' (Stewart, 2009a)

The use of analogy was undermined, here, on at least two counts. First, it was re-constructed as unduly flippant. Although the intention was to capitalise on a well-understood and well-known cultural reference, to help *explain* the concept of measurement inaccuracy, it was re-constructed as though the intention were to trivialise it, i.e. to *explain it away*, as though it could almost be laughed off. Clearly, examinations have serious impacts on students' life chances and should therefore not be trivialised. In contrast, the media report created an impression that explaining a serious matter through an entertainment analogy is somehow inherently disrespectful and trivialising.

Second, it was re-constructed as unduly ambivalent. Although the intention was to normalise the *fact* of error—since unreliability is generally recognised to be a feature of all human judgement—it was re-constructed as an attempt to trivialise the *extent* of error, which can be particularly extreme in English. This was achieved by linking two unrelated events, the analogy from Isabel Nisbet and the statement from Kathleen Tattersall, as though the two 'seem at odds' which, in fact, was not the case since there was no underlying contradiction. In retrospect, this attempt to normalise the inevitability of error in the context of an abnormal subject, English, proved to be a mistake, since it was linked to contemporaneous evidence of an unacceptable level of error in that subject. That is, the analogy was re-constructed as an attempt to excuse a particular instance of unacceptable misclassification rather than as an attempt to explain the general concept of misclassification. This was frustrating for a regulatory authority which believed in taking a strong stance against evidence of unacceptable error (Nisbet, personal communication, May 2012). The mistake was costly, since it proved to be an entertaining anecdote for subsequent assessment news stories to hark back to (e.g. Paton, 2009b). Indeed, when the Strictly Come Dancing analogy happened to be mentioned in a subsequent technical report from the Reliability Programme, Clark (2010a) made this the focus of her reporting.

The construction of evasiveness

Newton (2005a) explained why evidence of measurement inaccuracy does not necessarily imply that anyone is to blame. Although measurement inaccuracy *might* be caused by human error, there may be many causes that imply no such culpability. For instance, hay fever might prevent a student from performing on par, leading to a grade lower than that which they deserved, but not as a result of human error in any meaningful sense. On any account, this is just bad luck.

To address this linguistic challenge, researchers were contracted to investigate alternative ways of talking about error, with the intention of downplaying the apparent implication of culpability (Boyle *et al.*, 2009). The preferred term proved to be 'variation' which was chosen ahead of variance, uncertainty, discrepancy, inconsistency or clash. Unfortunately, once again, problems were encountered as this work was re-constructed by the media:

> JOBSWORTH education chiefs paid costly consultants to find new words for 'error' as it is considered 'too negative'.

> Exam watchdog Ofqual — set up to boost public confidence in qualifications — also admitted they avoid talking about the reliability of tests in case it causes bad publicity. (Charlton, 2009)

This time, the intention to improve public understanding was re-constructed as a desire to manipulate public confidence, by concealing error. In particular, notice how the acknowledgement that unreliability is a difficult topic because it 'seems like an intrinsically bad news story' (Boyle *et al.*, 2009, p. 1) was re-constructed in terms of Ofqual not wanting to talk about reliability in case it risked bad publicity, which has a far more sinister ring to it.

In separate coverage, the Chief Executive of the TaxPayer's Alliance was quoted as saying:

> This is a perfect example of where a quango has got so wrapped up in PR that it has started to neglect its real mission in favour of spin. If errors have been made, they should be called errors. (Paton, 2009b)

This quotation illustrates how precisely the wrong message was re-constructed from the Ofqual-sponsored research. Not only was it the explicit intention of Ofqual to avoid miscommunication, the whole point of the exercise was to find a way of conveying that unreliability does not necessarily mean that errors have been committed. Once more, to be fair to the report, it did close with a quotation from Ofqual to this effect. As was often the case, even sensationalist reporting typically contained important information and perspectives that might not otherwise have been aired.

Fanning the flames

The massive scale of national assessment, alongside the inevitability of measurement inaccuracy, means that problematic events need to be dealt with every year. Concerns were expressed within the examining community that the Reliability Programme would do little more than pour fuel on these simmering embers and fan the flames. Particular attention was therefore paid to the relationship between coverage of the Reliability Programme and coverage of events related to reliability that unfolded during its lifespan and subsequently. Did coverage of the Reliability Programme exacerbate system instability through associations drawn to ongoing events?

In fact, there seemed to be very little evidence of this. The three most significant parallel occurrences were:

(1) the failure of the national curriculum test marking system, which closely followed the launch of the programme (see Sutherland, 2008)
(2) the failure of part of the AQA script marking process toward the end of the programme (see Ofqual, 2011a), and
(3) the collection of examining board administration errors which followed the close of the programme (see Ofqual, 2011b).

Newspaper reporting of these occurrences did not appear to have been adversely affected by the Reliability Programme and, in the main, they were not linked to it at all. The same seemed to be true for reports of the release of data concerning National Curriculum test reviews and GCSE/A-level result enquiries, even when schools were expressing heightened concern over poorer quality marking than they had observed in previous years (e.g. Hurst, 2011; Paton, 2011).

One event did get linked to the Reliability Programme: the publication of research by academics at Bristol University, which was reported in March 2009 as 'Up to one in three children was given the wrong SATs grades last year amid a fiasco that triggered more than 200,000 appeals' (Clark, 2009). The story was associated with the Reliability Programme by Paton (2009c) and Stewart (2009b), both of whom regurgitated the Bristol research, six months later, whilst discussing the Ofqual presentation on talking about reliability (Boyle *et al.*, 2009). However, since no evidence was identified of the story being re-kindled beyond this coverage, it seems fair to conclude that this association did little to re-ignite the simmering embers of the Bristol research.

As a postscript, it is worth mentioning the events of summer 2012, which were also relevant. Following the publication of GCSE results, many schools expressed concern at outcomes for English. This was the first year in which grades had been awarded for a new suite of examinations in English and many schools had received a profile of results that seemed to be out-of-kilter with previous years, calling into question the reliability of those results. Ofqual investigated this anomaly and published a report (Ofqual, 2012). It claimed that standards had been applied correctly in the summer, although there had been problems in the design of the new qualifications, the examinations were now far less predictable than in previous years, and there was evidence that some teachers had inflated marks for internally-assessed components and that this had not been spotted during moderation. Once again, it is important to note that newspaper reporting of events did not hark back to outcomes from the Reliability Programme, so it could not be accused of having fanned the flames of this crisis either.

A measure of success

It is important to emphasise that there were plenty of fair-minded reports of research coming out of the Reliability Programme, i.e. ones that did not distort or mislead in the manner of the most sensational of those illustrated earlier (e.g. Mansell & Paton, 2009; Shepard, 2009; Stewart, 2009b, 2010). This was even true of media coverage of technical reports which presented data on levels of unre-liability of test and examination results—reports considered by many within the profession to be the most sensitive and therefore the most risky. For example, when research into the reliability of science tests was published, the *Telegraph* opened with the inevitable statement of 'bad news'—that between 12 and 17% of pupils were given the wrong results—and carried a quotation from the general secretary of the National Union of Teachers to the effect that these findings were worrying. Yet it ended with quotations from the Department for Children Schools and Families—intended to help normalise the inevitability of measurement inac-curacy—which presented the other side of the story:

> As Ofqual recognises, anyone who has taken tests or exams knows that external factors, like how a pupil feels on the day, can affect performance. (Paton, 2009c)

Although it was typical for coverage of reliability research to open with 'bad news' headlines such as 'One in five SATs results are incorrect' (Clark, 2010b) this should not be taken to mean that the coverage was necessarily unhelpful. Indeed, even 'bad news' headlines like this have the potential to improve public under-standing (assuming that they do not actually misrepresent the research) thereby helping to promulgate the message that error is inevitable. The risk, of course, is to public confidence. In this respect, it is interesting to note how the 'one in five' likelihood of incorrect results was constructed by Clark:

> But the findings will shake confidence in SATs in the week before national results are issued. (Clark, 2010b)

Thus, while the original research constructed 'one in five' as better than had previously been assumed (cf. Wiliam, 2001)—and therefore presented a 'good news' story of sorts—Clark (2010b) re-constructed it as a major threat to public confidence in National Curriculum testing (He *et al.*, 2011). The report therefore illustrates both the potential to improve public understanding through the promulgation of accurate estimates of unreliability, and the potential to damage public confidence through the creation of a template through which readers are invited to process the news, i.e. the 'shaking confidence' template. A similar template was presented by Collins (2010) under essentially the same headline:

> The figure was seized on by teaching leaders, who said the exams ought to be scrapped because they are not a reliable form of assessment for children. (Collins, 2010)

Of course, a template is only an invitation for the reader to process the news as implied by the reporter. Generally speaking, members of the public are not gullible and will reach their own judgements on the plausibility of the reporter's template. The fact that very few stories emerging from the Reliability Programme had legs, in the sense of being returned to time and time again and gathering their own head of steam, seemed to suggest that members of the public did not necessarily buy-into the most sensational aspects of the reporting.

Conclusions and discussion

Reports from the Reliability Programme were published and, in the main, the examining boards, test developers and regulator were not damned. This may only be an interim verdict, of course, but it is an encouraging indication all the same. Having said that, there should be no doubt that the Reliability Programme involved risks, since there were numerous examples of media reports in which attempts to improve public understanding were re-constructed as (more sensational and therefore more newsworthy) attempts to undermine public confidence or to bolster confidence unduly.

It seems, therefore, that the Reliability Programme may not have undermined public confidence unduly. What is not clear from this review of media coverage is whether it succeeded in its positive objective of improving public understanding. The fact that it attracted relatively little media attention is a good thing from the perspective of public confidence, signalling that the publication of research on unreliability was not sufficiently worrying to win extensive coverage. But it is a bad thing from the perspective of public understanding, since it necessarily reduces the potential positive impact. It seems fair to conclude that there is substantially more remaining be done to improve public understanding of reliability and error. Moreover, there are lessons to be learned from the Reliability Programme concerning ways in which this might, or might not, be achieved.

Lessons learned

Analogy is surely a powerful tool in the attempt to improve public understanding. Yet media coverage of the Strictly Come Dancing analogy revealed just how careful we need to be, to ensure that genuinely important concerns do not appear to be trivialised. Likewise, when faced with the most extreme examples of measurement inaccuracy, it may be prudent to resist the public understanding remit altogether, and to focus instead upon empathising with the apparent lack of public confidence.

Sensationalism is a double-edged sword for public understanding and confidence. On the one hand, a sensational story is likely to attract more readers, raising the potential for public understanding. On the other hand, if this sensationalism is achieved through exaggeration, selective reporting or misreporting, then this may threaten public understanding. Moreover, since sensationalism often rests upon a 'bad news' story, the threat to public confidence is always present.

In fact, even the most sensational and distorted reports on the Reliability Programme also contained a considerable amount of useful and informative coverage. Within the examining boards, it is sometimes felt that a 'bad news' along the lines of 'One in five SATs results are incorrect' (Clark, 2010b) is necessarily a problem, owing to the potential for threatening public confidence. Commenting on the way in which the media reported the Reliability Programme, the final report of the Policy Advisory Group expressed a similar concern:

> Whilst it is realised that the media always want to generate headlines that are interesting to their audience, Ofqual needs to develop a media handling strategy to alleviate the impact from such negative headlines on public confidence. (Burslem, 2011, p. 11)

Yet, if on balance the reporting is useful and informative—which it often proved to be—then it also has substantial potential to improve public understanding. Indeed, a 'bad news' headline on an otherwise useful and informative report might be precisely the balance sought, with the overt sensationalism helping to draw readers in. Of course, this assumes that more than the headline is actually read, which will not always be the case.

Normalising measurement inaccuracy

Launching the Reliability Programme entailed picking up the gauntlet dropped by academics such as Black *et al.* (2007). At a practical level, it led to new insights concerning operational levels of reliability; for instance, the conclusion that the 30% misclassification estimate from Wiliam (2001) was a substantial over-estimate. At a more emblematic level, however, it represented a new commitment to normalising the concept of measurement inaccuracy in educational assessment; that is, a commitment to helping members of the public to understand the inevitability of measurement inaccuracy and to distinguish between reports of measurement inaccuracy that are newsworthy and those which are not. Normalising the concept of measurement inaccuracy will entail a commitment to the ongoing, routine production of evidence of unreliability. As more and more evidence is made public, it will become less and less feasible for media reports to sensationalise measurement inaccuracy, other than when indefensible abnormal cases come to light that might deserve to be sensationalised.

The importance of this process of normalisation through the routine publication of evidence of unreliability should not be underestimated. As mentioned earlier, the issue is not whether members of the public genuinely believe that error exists, it is whether they can be constructed as believing this, in media reports, and whether the examining boards can be constructed as guilty of error and of concealing it. These media constructions have the power to damage and destabilise, independently of what individuals might 'actually believe' from one moment to the next. Yet constructions like this only stand a chance of influencing the tide of public opinion if they contain at least a grain of truth. The more obviously false a media construction, the less likely it will be selected for publication in the first place, and the less impact it would have if it were to be published. As such, the larger the corpus of evidence of unreliability that is routinely published the better.

The very idea of error

The experience of running the Reliability Programme revealed very clearly that it failed to establish an effective lexicon for communicating the central ideas of measurement inaccuracy. The studies of Strand 1 set out to investigate a narrow technical concept called reliability, which is well established in the literature and which has a precise meaning. In fact, as the final report of the Technical Advisory Group pointed out, even reliability has a number of different meanings in the literature and there is no consensus over the best way to model it (see Baird *et al.*, 2011, p. 19). Broader than reliability, however, was the concept of measurement inaccuracy, which was described more informally as error. Whether it was appropriate to talk in terms of 'error' proved to be a major bone of contention.

Error... or just variability?

The Technical Advisory Group preferred the term 'unwanted variability' to error. According to them, the 'truth' about a student's level of attainment is ultimately unknowable—indeed there may actually be no 'truth' about it—which means that it is problematic to speak of error. Boyle *et al.* (2009) preferred the term 'variation'.

Although the idea of unwanted variability is attractive, it may not help greatly with improving public understanding. It seems to invoke the concept of construct-irrelevant variance from the technical literature on validity, i.e. the variation in a set of assessment results that is not attributable to genuine differences between students in the attribute being assessed. On the one hand, this is a tricky concept for even assessment professionals to understand, and the new name does little to clarify it. On the other hand, even construct-irrelevant variance invokes the idea of a genuine level of attainment that is not reflected in the assessment result. So the need to invoke error does not go away. The Technical Advisory Group wished to emphasise that whether an essay deserved a score of 15 versus 16 could not have an unequivocally correct answer, so the concept of error was problematic. Yet, the more extreme the variation observed, the less problematic the concept of error becomes. And there are always instances of human error that indisputably result in measurement inaccuracy error, e.g. large 'clerical' errors in recording marks. In short, we cannot avoid invoking the concept of error, even if it can sometimes be parsed as variability. Indeed, the whole point of evaluating unreliability is to reach a conclusion as to whether there is so much variability that we can no longer treat assessment results as sufficiently accurate.

Essentially the same response could be made to Boyle *et al.* (2009). Although variation may well be a better term to use than reliability, it is no substitute for measurement inaccuracy, which means that it cannot substitute for error. When reports on unreliability make it into the media they tend to be associated with constructions such as the following:

- one in five students is awarded the wrong grade, or
- 30% of students may be given the wrong level.

These constructions are undoubtedly appropriate and sensible. They express in commonsense language the idea that a certain percentage of students will not be awarded a result that represents their true level of attainment, i.e. the idea that the Ofqual definition of exam error was meant to capture for Strands 2 and 3. Finessing this, with the recognition that some measurement inaccuracy is nothing more than legitimate variability, makes for an interesting academic debate. But it is not going to help public understanding, since there will be plenty of measurement inaccuracy that is not so easily dismissed.

Error... and culpability?

While the concept of error was fundamental to the Reliability Programme, the use of the term was undoubtedly problematic. It was not simply a problem for participants in Strand 3 studies (e.g. Ipsos Mori, 2009; Chamberlain, 2010), it also proved to be a problem for us, the researchers! When planning Strand 3, Ofqual attempted to explain the concept of error as simply as possible: as a difference between the grade that a student *should* have been awarded, on the basis of their level of attainment at the time of the examination, and the grade that they *actually* were awarded.

In order to set the scene for participants, during one of the earliest studies, a research team reconstructed the Ofqual concept of exam error as though, for instance, Ofqual considered illness and stress to be error, in contrast to most members of the public who would see them as simply bad luck. In effect, the researchers had misrepresented the Ofqual definition. Illness and stress may well be genuine *causes* of error (a.k.a. measurement inaccuracy) but they could not meaningfully be called errors in their own right. At other points, the research team correctly employed the Ofqual definition, but went on to attribute this measurement inaccuracy to further errors in the assessment process. Again, the researchers had almost understood, but not entirely, since measurement inaccuracy will arise even in the absence of procedural error. The study was not in vain, since it still generated substantial evidence of public perceptions, and misperceptions; yet it failed to enable participants to engage with the Ofqual definition of error.

What appeared to confuse this research team, as well as their participants, was the distinction between error-as-incorrect-claim and error-as-procedural-violation. In the former, the examination result makes a claim about a student's level of attainment, that happens to be incorrect. In the latter, something has occurred to cause that claim to be incorrect, and it is this procedural violation that is referred to as the error rather than, or in addition to, the claim. Under the Ofqual definition, error referred only to the former (the incorrect claim) even though it may also have been caused by the latter (an adverse event). This is clearly a very tricky concept for even researchers to grasp, let alone their participants. It is even more confusing since human error may well be a cause of measurement inaccuracy; although, as the examples of illness and stress make clear, human error need not be to blame after all.

The outstanding challenge

The Reliability Programme resulted in the publication of a body of important new research related to public understanding of, and confidence in, public examinations; including research into the reporting of error and uncertainty, and into communicating with the public about measurement inaccuracy (Opposs & He, 2012). In addition, as described above, important insights into the potential for improving public understanding and confidence arose from the ways in which Reliability Programme outcomes and agents were re-constructed through media reporting. Unfortunately, the programme failed to deliver on one of its central aims, which was to establish an effective language through which to communicate with members of the public about reliability. Unless this challenge is confronted directly, the potential for improving public understanding and confidence is unlikely to be realised.

Reliability is a technical concept, in fact a very abstruse technical concept, with little real-world significance. More fundamental, and with more real-world significance, is the broader concept of measurement inaccuracy, the difference between results being accurate or inaccurate. Yet neither reliability nor measurement inaccuracy are user-friendly terms and the term error proved to carry too much baggage. As a closing thought, one way to address this challenge might be to draw clearer distinctions between two separate conversations. The first is a conversation about measurement inaccuracy, for which we might speak simply in terms of the likelihood of students getting the 'right grade' or the 'wrong grade'.[2] This is the language of media reporting, which provides good reason to think that it is targeted appropriately. The second is a conversation about culpability, for which the focus need not be upon quantification at all, but upon the causes and impacts of measurement inaccuracy and upon the critical issue of blame.

Acknowledgements

This paper was produced with the support of my employer, Cambridge Assessment, although the views expressed are entirely my own. I would like to thank Andrew Boyle, Isabel Nisbet, Dennis Opposs and John Gardner for very helpful comments on earlier drafts.

Notes

1. While the term reliability has a narrow technical meaning which is generally accepted, there is no generally accepted term to express the overall error that has been described here as measurement inaccuracy. In Newton (2005a), I distinguished 'measurement inaccuracy' (i.e. error as the difference between correct and incorrect assessment result) from 'human error' (i.e. error as the violation of an assessment procedure). I described both as aspects of 'assessment error'. There is no clear relationship between measurement inaccuracy and human error since measurement inaccuracy can (and will) arise in the absence of human error, and human error may not actually result in measurement inaccuracy.
2. This will requires the translation of reliability statistics into classification accuracy statistics, with the proviso that these are likely to be underestimates.

References

Baird, J., Beguin, A., Black, P., Pollitt, A. & Stanley, G. (2011). *The Reliability Programme: final report of the technical advisory group*. Ofqual/11/4825. Coventry, Ofqual.

Black, P., Gardner, J. & Wiliam, D. (2007). Joint memorandum, in: House of Commons Children, Schools and Families Committee *Testing and Assessment. Third Report of session 2007–08. Volume II. Oral and written evidence*. HC 169-II (Ev.202-205). London, The Stationery Office.

Black, B., Suto, I. & Bramley, T. (2011). The interrelations of features of questions, mark schemes and examinee responses and their impact upon marker agreement. *Assessment in Education: Principles, Policy & Practice*, 18(3), 295–318.

Boyle, A., Opposs, D. & Kinsella, A. (2009). No news is good news? Talking to the public about the reliability of assessment. Ofqual/09/4362. Paper presented at the *35th International Association for Educational Assessment (IAEA) Annual Conference*, Brisbane, 13–18 September. Coventry, Ofqual.

Burslem, S. (2011). *The Reliability Programme. Final report of the Policy Advisory Group*. Ofqual/11/4829. Coventry, Ofqual.

Chamberlain, S. (2010). *Public perceptions of reliability. Ofqual/10/4708.* Coventry, Ofqual.

Charlton, J. (2009, 18 September). No room for error in exams. *Sun.*

Clark, L. (2009, 18 March). One in three children is given wrong grade for SATs every year. *MailOnline.*

Clark, L. (2010a, 6 February). Strictly come marking: As 1 in 3 pupils get wrong grade, SATs are branded as unreliable as TV show judging. *MailOnline.*

Clark, L. (2010b, 27 July). One in five SATs results are incorrect. *Daily Mail.*

Collins, N. (2010, 26 July). One in five pupils receive wrong Sats grade. *Telegraph.*

Crisp, V. (2008). Exploring the nature of examiner thinking during the process of examination marking. *Cambridge Journal of Education*, 38(2), 247–264.

Crisp, V. & Johnson, M. (2007). The use of annotations in examination marking: opening a window into markers' minds. *British Educational Research Journal*, 33(6), 943–961.

Edgeworth, F.Y. (1888). The statistics of examinations. *Journal of the Royal Statistical Society*, LI, 599-635.

Greatorex, J. & Bell, J.F. (2004). Does the gender of examiners influence their marking? *Research in Education*, 71, 25–36.

Hartog, P. & Rhodes, E.C. (1935). *An examination of examinations.* London, Macmillan.

He, Q., Boyle, A. & Opposs, D. (2011). Public perceptions of reliability in examination results in England. *Evaluation & Research in Education*, 24(4), 255–283.

He, Q. & Opposs, D. (2011). The reliability of results from national tests, public examinations, and vocational qualifications in England. *Educational Research and Evaluation*, 18(8), 779–799.

House of Commons Children, Schools and Families Committee (2008). *Testing and assessment. Third report of session 2007–08. Volume II. Oral and written evidence. HC 169-II.* London, TSO Ltd.

Hurst, G. (2011, 8 December). Thousands of A-level results upgraded as complaints soar. *The Times.*

Ipsos MORI (2009). *Public perceptions of reliability in examinations: A research study conducted for Ofqual.* Coventry, Ofqual.

Lawn, M. (Ed.) (2008). *An Atlantic crossing? The work of the International Examinations Inquiry, its researchers, methods and influence.* Oxford, Symposium Books.

Mansell, W. & Paton, G. (2009, 12 May). Exam grades 'should be scrapped'. *Telegraph.co.uk.*

Mansell, W. (2003, 17 October). Test result bombshell kept under wraps. *The Times Educational Supplement.*

Mansell, W. (2006, 18 August). Persistent professor returns. *The Times Educational Supplement.*

Murphy, R.J.L. (1978). Reliability of marking in eight GCE examinations, *British Journal of Educational Psychology*, 48, 196–200.

Newton, P.E. (1996). The reliability of marking of General Certificate of Secondary Education Scripts: mathematics and English. *British Educational Research Journal*, 22(4), 405–420.

Newton, P.E. (2005a). The public understanding of measurement inaccuracy, *British Educational Research Journal*, 31(4), 419–442.

Newton, P.E. (2005b). Threats to the professional understanding of assessment error, *Journal of Education Policy*, 20(4), 457–483.

Newton, P.E. (2007). Contextualising the comparability of examination standards, in: P.E. Newton, J. Baird, H. Goldstein, H. Patrick & P. Tymms (Eds) *Techniques for monitoring the comparability of examination standards.* London, Qualifications and Curriculum Authority.

Newton, P. E. (2008a). Recognising the error of our ways. Paper presented at the *Cambridge Assessment Forum for New Developments in Educational Assessment.* Downing College, Cambridge, 10 December.

Newton, P. E. (2008b). Ofqual's reliability of results programme. Paper presented at the *Association of Colleges Annual Conference (Changing Landscapes)*. International Convention Centre, Birmingham, 18–20 November.

Newton, P.E. (2011). A-level pass rates and the enduring myth of norm-referencing. *Research Matters, Special Issue*, 2, 20–26.

Ofqual (2011a). Inquiry into the failure of part of AQA's GCSE, AS and A-level script-marking process in the summer 2010 examination series. Coventry, Ofqual.

Ofqual (2011b, 4 August). Action taken on exam errors. Available online at: http://www.ofqual. gov.uk/news-and-announcements/130-news-and-announcements-press-releases/720-action-taken-on-exam-errors.

Ofqual (2012). *GCSE English 2012*. Coventry, Ofqual.

Opposs, D. & He, Q. (2011). *The Reliability Programme. Final report. Ofqual/11/4828*. Coventry, Ofqual.

Opposs, D. & He, Q. (2011). *Ofqual's reliability compendium*. Coventry, Ofqual.

Paton, G. (2009a, 30 January). Exam marking errors 'inevitable', says regulator. *Telegraph.co.uk*.

Paton, G. (2009b). Exam watchdog bans 'errors'. *Telegraph.co.uk*, 18 September.

Paton, G. (2009c, 13 November). Sats results 'wrong for thousands of pupils'. *Telegraph.co.uk*.

Paton, G. (2011, 8 December). Record number of A-levels marked up amid scramble for university places. *The Daily Telegraph*.

Petch, J.A. (1953). *Fifty years of examining*. London, Harrap.

Roach, J. (1971). *Public examinations in England 1850–1900*. London, Cambridge University Press.

Ross, T. (2009, 31 January). New Sats fiasco as one in three pupils 'will get wrong exam results'. *MailOnline*.

Shepard, J. (2009, 22 December). Exam results could carry inaccuracy warning. *Guardian.co.uk*.

Stewart, W. (2009a, 27 March). Ofqual chief wrong-footed in marking row. *The Times Educational Supplement*.

Stewart, W. (2009b, 18 September). Exams: Ofqual admits to 'shying away' from talking about test result reliability. *The Times Educational Supplement*.

Stewart, W. (2010, 19 March). Primary teachers have 'almost blind faith' in grades. *The Times Educational Supplement*.

Sutherland, S. (2008). *The Sutherland Inquiry: an independent inquiry into the delivery of National Curriculum tests in 2008. A report to Ofqual and the Secretary of State for Children, Schools and Families*. London, The Stationery Office.

Suto, W.M.I. & Greatorex, J. (2008). A quantitative analysis of cognitive strategy usage in the marking of two GCSE examinations. *Assessment in Education: Principles, Policy & Practice*, 15(1), 73–89.

Suto, W.M.I. & Greatorex, J. (2008). What goes through an examiner's mind? Using verbal protocols to gain insights into the GCSE marking process. *British Educational Research Journal*, 34(2), 213–233.

Tattersall, K. (2007). A brief history of policies, practices and issues relating to comparability, in: P.E. Newton, J. Baird, H. Goldstein, H. Patrick & P. Tymms (Eds) *Techniques for monitoring the comparability of examination standards*. London, Qualifications and Curriculum Authority.

Tattersall, K. (2008). Speech at Ofqual Launch Event, National Motorcycle Museum. Solihull, 16 May.

Warmington, P. & Murphy, R. (2004) Could do better? Media depictions of UK educational assessment results. *Journal of Education Policy*, 19(3), 285–299.

Wiliam, D. (2001). Reliability, validity, and all that jazz. *Education, 3–13*, 29(3), 17–21.

Wiseman, S. (1961) The efficiency of examinations, in: S. Wiseman (Ed.) *Examinations in education*. Manchester, Manchester University Press.

Communication strategies for enhancing qualification users' understanding of educational assessment: recommendations from other public interest fields

Suzanne Chamberlain

Centre for Education Research & Policy, Assessment & Qualifications Alliance, Manchester, UK

The outcomes of national assessments in many countries provide 'qualifications' or 'credentials' that may be used to define the levels of students' knowledge and skills, for their own use and that of employers, higher education institutions and others. Qualification users, such as students, parents and teachers, arguably need to have an understanding of some basic principles of educational assessment in order to make informed judgements about the reliability of assessment outcomes, and to develop realistic expectations of what assessment systems can deliver. The goal of achieving this has gathered pace recently with the completion of a two-year research programme in England that explored concerns around technical aspects of assessment and current levels of public understanding of assessment. One of the recommendations of the programme was that qualification awarding bodies should collect and make available information relating to the reliability of outcomes for various types of qualification. Further consideration is required, however, to determine what, and how much, assessment information would be useful to qualification users, and how it might best be presented and disseminated. As a contribution to this process, this paper discusses the communication strategies employed in other fields for the purpose of sharing important messages with the public. Three recommendations are offered for overcoming some of the challenges inherent in improving communication and understanding of assessment. The paper concludes that enhancing qualification users' understanding of assessment may be achieved by focusing on the presentation of applied, interpretive information and dissemination through influential peers from various stakeholder groups.

Background: public understanding of assessment

Presently, the three awarding bodies offering national qualifications at the end of compulsory and non-compulsory schooling in England[1] do not routinely publish, in the wider public domain, measures of the quality and performance of the examinations and assessments that they offer. Psychometric analyses of performance, and other measures of assessment quality, tend to be used as part of internal quality assurance processes and to inform the development of subsequent assessments. Typically, they are not shared with the public or discussed in the public domain. As such, qualification users tend to be unaware of the extent to which the reliability of assessment outcomes (scores and grades) varies across subjects and different modes of assessment (e.g. essay-based exams, multiple-choice tests, oral tests, coursework), and within subjects over time (e.g. Bramley & Dhawan, 2012). Qualification users may also be unaware of how grade reliability is influenced by other key assessment design features, such as the number of assessment occasions, the length of tests, question type and quality, how questions are sampled from different content areas, the number of grade distinctions available, and the standard setting method (e.g. Betebenner *et al.* 2008; Johnson & Johnson, 2012; Wheadon & Stockford, 2012).

Assessment and assessment results serve multiple purposes (see Newton, 2007), and it is essential to be clear about the intended audiences and purpose(s) of any efforts to release assessment information. The term 'assessment information' is used in this paper to refer to assessment concepts and principles, and empirical evidence of the performance of students or assessment instruments, as it is likely that efforts to enhance public understanding will draw upon different aspects of assessment information. A distinction is therefore made in this paper between two types of audience: 'qualification users' and the general 'public'. The former refers to the groups of individuals who have direct relations to the outputs of the assessment system, such as teachers, students, parents, higher education admissions tutors and employers. The term 'qualification user' prioritises individuals' relations with educational assessment, but it is recognised that such groups are diverse and other socio-educational distinctions may carry more weight in determining their responses to and interest in assessment information. The 'public' is used to refer generically to laypeople who, it may be assumed, have no specialist interest in, or specialist understanding of, assessment.

The Office of Qualifications and Examinations Regulation (Ofqual) has taken an active role in exploring whether the current situation in England should be addressed by encouraging the publication of reliability and other assessment information. Ofqual commissioned a two-year research programme consisting of a series of studies on the topic of the reliability of national examination and test results (see Ofqual, 2009). The studies were concerned with the technical measurement of reliability (e.g. Johnson & Johnson, 2012; Wheadon & Stockford, 2012), and public perceptions of the reliability of examination and test results in England (Chamberlain, 2012a; He *et al.*, 2012; Johnson *et al.*, 2012). These studies formed the evidence base for a set of initial recommendations on the collection and dissemination of reliability and related information by qualification awarding bodies (see Baird *et al.*, 2012; Burslem, 2012; Opposs & He, 2012a). One of the final reports on the research programme recommended that qualification awarding bodies should be encouraged to 'generate and publish reliability information', and improve public understanding of assessment reliability, including helping the public to interpret reliability evidence (Burslem, 2012, pp. 850–851). Some of the challenges inherent to this task were acknowledged in the detail of the recommendations. For example, the recommendations referred to the use of plain language, providing explanations of technical terms and the factors that introduce inconsistency in educational measurement, and utilising analogies from other fields (Burslem, 2012; Opposs & He, 2012b). As reliability is only one measure of assessment quality, a similar programme on 'Assessment Validity' commenced in 2012 with the aim of establishing a framework for collecting and evaluating evidence of the validity of national assessments (see Ofqual, 2012). Should this preliminary work on reliability and validity produce mandatory requirements for the collection and publication of assessment information, there is potentially a wealth of information that could be shared with qualification users and the general public.

The pitfalls and benefits of enhancing communication about assessment

The potential impacts of enhancing qualification users' understanding of assessment and, in particular, the levels of uncertainty associated with various forms of assessment, are not fully understood. On one hand, it is conceivable that increasing awareness of the uncertainty inherent in educational measurement may undermine confidence in the outcomes of the national assessment system. Research suggests that qualification users (with the exception of teachers) tend to be satisfied that examination grades and scores are accurate measures of ability which are mostly consistent with their perceptions of what was deserved (e.g. Chamberlain, 2012a, 2012b). As there are no public 'proofs' of trustworthiness (O'Neill, 2002), qualification users may understandably have a naïve trust in assessment outcomes. Trust and confidence in the system may therefore be threatened by publicising the fact that grades may be more or less reliable, depending on the assessment context.

On the other hand, Newton (2005) argues that enhancing public understanding of assessment will not diminish confidence, but that it is, in fact, essential to the fostering of confidence in the assessment system. Informing the public of what the system can and cannot realistically deliver will prevent it being held accountable for limitations that may be perceived as human failings, but which are actually inherent to educational measurement. It would also encourage qualification users to develop more informed interpretations of assessment outcomes (Newton, 2005). This would be particularly pertinent to those who use grades and scores to make important selection decisions in education and employment. An understanding of basic assessment principles may encourage selectors to view assessment outcomes as 'approximations' (Murphy, 2004) or 'estimates' (Harlen, 1994) of ability that are products of particular assessment environments, rather than incontrovertible facts. Allowing qualification users to access information about the quality and reliability of the qualifications which they purchase, teach, study or use, is also consistent with the tenets of a transparent and just society (Giddens, 1990).

The educational assessment community is not unique in wishing to share complex information with the public and to enhance public understanding, nor is it unique in having hurdles to overcome in doing so. This paper looks to other public interest fields for guidance on the strategies that could be employed to share complex information with the public and enhance public understanding. Of particular interest here are the questions relating to how information can be presented to generate interest in assessment and how it could be disseminated to maximum effect. Three recommendations are made: two relating to the presentation of information and one relating to dissemination. Given that they are somewhat counter to current industry practices, it is to be expected that they may prove challenging to implement. However, there is increasing recognition that the assessment community should share information with qualification users (Newton, 2005; Ofqual, 2009), and it therefore is important to assess their potential utility critically. It is also worth considering implementing communication strategies while, currently, traditional written examinations remain the dominant mode of assessment. Emerging forms of assessment, such as on-screen, on-demand or adaptive testing, may in time become commonplace, and introduce new and potentially more complex matters, such as test equating, to the debates (e.g. Wheadon *et al.*, 2009).

The challenges of communicating about educational assessment

There is not space in this paper to consider the literature on challenges of communicating assessment information publicly in other countries, but the United States provides pertinent examples of how the matters are addressed. For example, in some states assessors are required by law to produce reliability and other assessment information for qualification users and the general public (Goodman & Hambleton, 2004; Hattie, 2010; Phelps *et al.*, 2012). Where there is no legal obligation, testing agencies and test publishers tend to abide, in any case, by the guidance given in the *Standards for educational and psychological testing* (American Educational Research Association, American Psychological Association, National Council on Measurement in Education, 1999), which also advocates the publication of a range of reliability measures for scores at various levels of aggregation (Phelps *et al.*, 2012). However, a number of studies have found that readers of the reports on US assessment results find them confusing and difficult to interpret (see Goodman & Hambleton, 2004). Examples of the criticisms are that they contain a significant amount of technical jargon and statistical symbols, they refer to concepts unfamiliar to readers and are presented within text that tends to be dense (Goodman & Hambleton, 2004; Hattie, 2010). The reports on the California High School Exit

Exam (e.g. Becker *et al.*, 2011), for example, tend to be several hundred pages long (Phelps *et al.*, 2012), and refer to complex analyses such as test equating and inter-rater reliability. Although useful headline findings are provided, such as 'Test scores have been improving' and 'Significant gaps in passing rates persist' (Becker *et al.*, 2011, p. 3), the reports are arguably presented with the specialist, rather than lay, audience in mind.

Simply releasing information into the public domain is not sufficient to ensure that those for whom the information matters will locate it or (be able to) engage with it (O'Neill, 2002). Similarly, Nisbet (2009) claims that increasing media coverage of a particular concern will not guarantee 'more' understanding, or that the information will 'speak for itself' or be interpreted by all audiences in the intended way. Indeed, Giddens (1990) suggests it is unrealistic to expect much more of lay-persons than an ambivalence towards technical knowledge, as it is only through longer periods of 'study' that individuals are exposed to arguments about the fallibility of particular bodies of knowledge.

Goodman and Hambleton (2004) offer some recommendations for improving the accessibility of results reports in the USA. These include the importance of clear, uncluttered presentation, avoidance of statistical terms, and providing text to support the interpretations of charts. The recommendations represent good industry practices. However, it is possible to add to their list by looking beyond educational assessment to other industries and professionals who have attempted to communicate complex issues to the public. In doing so, this paper offers three additional recommendations:

Relating to the presentation of information, the recommendations are to:

- Develop educational assessment frames
- Use applied and interpretive information, not description and explanation

Relating to disseminating information and engaging qualification users, the recommendation is to:

- Recruit influential peers from assessment stakeholder groups as information brokers

These recommendations have been drawn from the literature on communicating climate change, the findings of health risk studies (specifically related to the combined Measles-Mumps-Rubella (MMR) vaccine), and public understanding of science. Clearly, these are very complex matters of public import, with underlying political, moral and public educational agendas that have determined processes and events around them. However, arguably central to all of them is the extent to which the public is in possession of the relevant facts and have developed the necessary understanding to grapple with the challenges presented. The examples have been selected on the basis that they replicate and address these similar concerns in educational assessment: namely, how to make complex information accessible and interesting to non-specialists, and how to disseminate the information to a diverse range of stakeholders. The first recommendation is drawn from a review of the communication of climate change policy, and proposes a method for the presentation of complex information. The second is based on lessons learnt following the MMR vaccination controversy in the late 1990s, and emphasises that the presentation of information should be driven by the needs of the intended audience. The final recommendation is also drawn from the climate change literature but is rationalised with reference to the comprehensive programme of initiatives to improve public understanding of science. It proposes a method for the dissemination of information that places the intended users at the heart of the dissemination process, and eschews traditional top-down or media-reliant approaches.

Educational assessment is a high profile, high stakes industry that attracts significant media attention, and this phenomenon is clearly articulated in Warmington and Murphy (2004, 2007). Any communication about educational assessment therefore requires careful consideration (e.g. Baird *et al.*, 2012). There is perhaps as much potential for negative media attention as there is for positive public engagement (see Boyle *et al.*, 2012). Some risks and limitations associated with the recommendations are also discussed.

Recommendation 1: Develop educational assessment frames

Nisbet (2009, p. 16) reviews the communication of climate change policy in the USA, a topic which he labels 'the ultimate ambiguous situation given its complexity and perceived uncertainty'. Previous efforts to enhance understanding of climate change were considered unsuccessful as they focused on simply increasing the volume of media output which was likely to appeal only to a small audience of those with an interest in the subject. Instead, Nisbet emphasises the importance of using frames to enhance public understanding. A frame is a means of simplifying and contextualising (technical) information, and may consist of metaphors, allusions, examples and carefully constructed sound bites that trigger new ways of thinking about and applying information (Fisher, 1997; Nisbet, 2009). A well constructed frame helps to make complex information understandable, relevant and personally important, while maintaining truthfulness and accuracy about the topic in question (Nisbet, 2009). Frames referring to climate change have included the 'pollution paradigm', which stressed the detrimental environmental impacts associated with greenhouse gas emissions, and the more recent 'economic development' frame, in which climate change is promoted as a rationale for economic action and growth through the development of environmentally-friendly products and processes (Nordhaus & Schellenberger, 2007; cited in Nisbet, 2009). In England, familiar climate change frames have included 'going green', which refers to the take up of environmentally-aware behaviours and practices in industry (e.g. Dale, 2008), and 'clean energy' to promote the benefits and use of different forms of natural and renewable energy (Department of Energy and Climate Change, 2012).

In educational assessment, frames could be developed to introduce key assessment concepts and serve as primers to the release of more complex information such as reliability statistics for various qualifications. The use of frames may help educational assessors to present assessment information without reference to technical terms such as reliability, validity or error, which can be confused with their everyday meanings (e.g. Burslem, 2012). Indeed, as part of the Ofqual reliability research programme, the potential utility of alternative terms to error was explored in an effort to increase the accessibility of the language of assessment reliability. The terms included variance, variation, discrepancy and uncertainty, with 'variation' considered the most appropriate (Boyle *et al.*, 2012). The final technical report of the Ofqual programme favoured 'unwanted variability' to refer to the 'variability which is not associated with what the test is trying to measure' (Baird *et al.*, 2012, p. 786). Arguably, these terms are as equally technical as 'reliability'. Further work would be required to construct suitable frames for assessment, but they may include assessment 'quality', 'trustworthiness', 'dependability', 'how to interpret your grade', 'what your grade means', or other frames that make abstract assessment concepts understandable and meaningful to non-specialists.

There are, however, risks involved in simplifying complex information and relying on sound bites and analogies, and frames may be vulnerable to misinterpretation. In discussing the release to the news media of the results of health risk studies, Riesch and Spiegelhalter (2011) show how vagueness can lead to sensationalised (mis-)reporting as news reporters draw their own interpretations or develop their own frames. One notable example was the media emphasis on the 'dangers' of popular foods such as bacon sandwiches and hot dogs following the release of study findings in 2007 relating to the causes of cancer and which advised 'moderate' consumption of processed meats (see Riesch & Spiegelhalter, 2011).

Frames may not find favour with educational assessors as sound bites may be perceived as crudely simplistic (Warmington & Murphy, 2004) and may leave educational assessors vulnerable to media criticism. This is exemplified by media responses to the release of A-level results (a post-compulsory qualification typically used for entry to Higher Education) in England each summer. An increase in the pass rate over successive years has been presented in a 'falling standards' frame that is profitable for journalists, in terms of generating interesting news coverage, but frustrating for educational assessors, and others, who seek to defend the value of the A-level qualification (Warmington & Murphy, 2004, 2007). Frames may also be used to publicise particular political, economic or social ideologies. The term 'climate change' is in itself a frame that emerged in response to claims that the frame 'global warming' did not capture the scientific uncertainty about climate change, was 'frightening', and was associated with environmentalists who, in the USA, were perceived as extremists (e.g. Burkeman, 2003). These limitations should be balanced against the potential for offering qualification users a means by which they can, if they wish, side-step the underpinning assessment concepts and technical terminology, while still gaining access to important information.

Recommendation 2: Use applied and interpretive information, not description and explanation

In 1998 a research paper described the onset of regressive autism in eight children following receipt of the MMR vaccine (Wakefield *et al.*, 1998; cited in Offit & Coffin, 2003). Although the paper was later retracted, it generated significant news media coverage which, in turn, prompted a fall in the MMR vaccination rate in the UK, with concern also spreading to the USA (Offit & Coffin, 2003). A significant part of the post-controversy analysis was to understand the chains of communication, and understand what types of information were persuasive in parents' decisions to consent to, or refuse, the vaccine for their children. As part of this, it has been noted that, in this instance, parents favoured and were more likely to respond to informal, rather than formal, sources and types of information.

In the MMR case, media reports of the scientific evidence of the relationship between the vaccine and autism were claimed to be of less interest and play a lesser role in parents' decision-making, than other forms of information. Petts and Niemeyer (2004) found, for example, that parents preferred to discuss the risks associated with the vaccine in face-to-face interactions with health professionals, while Offit and Coffin (2003) emphasised the usefulness of other parents' perspectives and personal experiences of the vaccine. Parents' beliefs about the vaccine and their responses to the controversy (consenting to their children being vaccinated, or not) tended to be more influenced by information that was directly applicable to their own lives than other forms of information (e.g. Bellaby, 2003; Offit & Coffin, 2003; Petts & Niemeyer, 2004).

Offit and Coffin (2003) outline that MMR media coverage tended to focus on emotive, dramatic and personal stories of parents who believed their children had been harmed by the vaccine. It is claimed that study findings that showed there was no causal relationship between the vaccine and autism were neglected in the USA, as they did not contain personal accounts, and interpreting findings would have required complex, technical explanations of methods and analyses (Offit & Coffin, 2003). Instead, the personal stories were an interesting source of information that provided parents with a framework to apply the debates about the risks of the vaccine to the lives of their own children (Bellaby, 2003). Crucially, they were also a trusted source, as information was conferred from parent to parent, while official or scientific sources were treated with some suspicion (Bellaby, 2003). Offit and Coffin (2003) discuss the reasons why, in this case, the scientific information may have been unpersuasive or unengaging. Among other reasons, they note that 'Out of respect for the scientific method, aware of the fact that one cannot accept the null hypothesis, and mindful of the limits imposed by the size of epidemiologic studies, we do not say "MMR vaccine *does not* cause autism". However, neither the media nor the public may understand the reasons for our reticence' (Offit & Coffin, 2003, p. 4, emphasis added). The scientists no doubt reported and discussed their findings in ways appropriate to their scientific norms (i.e. being precise and accurate). However, this did not seemingly curry favour with the general public—in the same way, perhaps, that psychometric reports on assessment results in the USA tend to alienate potential readers with technical jargon and statistical symbols (Goodman & Hambleton, 2004).

The final report of the Ofqual Reliability of Results programme suggests that the following information should be shared with the general public: explanations of technical terms, how the assessment system works, the factors that can influence the consistency of outcomes, and information on understanding and interpreting reliability information, such as Cronbach's alpha coefficients (Burslem, 2012; Opposs & He, 2012b). In the light of the public's responses to the formal and informal information on the MMR vaccine, it may be of benefit to consider whether this breadth of information is necessary. Formal descriptions of assessment terminology and explanations of concepts may not be the type of information that is likely to engage the intended audience. Instead, educational assessors may wish to explore ways of prioritising interpretations of information, and presenting interpretations that stress, or provide examples of, how the information is directly applicable to the individual. Tufte (e.g. 2001) provides numerous examples of simple graphical displays of different types of quantitative information that may also stimulate ideas for the presentation of reliability data.

Indeed, Salvagno and Teglasi (1987) found support among teachers for interpretive information over factual or descriptive information in reports of test results, with teachers expressing a preference for specific guidelines on how to apply information to their own contexts. Similarly, Hattie (2010) argues that teachers should not be expected to learn the language of educational assessors; instead, educational assessors should learn the language of teachers. Teachers' priorities are focused on teaching, learning and classroom practices, and they will want to know how assessment information can be applied in that context (Hattie, 2010).

Recommendation 3: Recruit influential peers to act as information brokers

Initiatives to enhance public understanding of science in the UK have drawn attention to the fact that scientists are not necessarily skilled in communicating with the media or public (e.g. The Royal Society, 1985; House of Lords, 2000). Early claims that scientists' efforts to communicate were hindered by the public's inability to understand scientific concepts, a disinterest in science, and acrimonious relations with the media were discredited (Gregory, 2001). Instead, it was recognised that scientific institutions tended to set themselves apart from wider society and efforts to share scientific information tended to be self-serving for the scientists involved (House of Lords, 2000; Gregory, 2001). The public's trust in scientists has also been undermined at times by crises such as the epidemic of 'mad cow disease', during which the public were ill-advised by the government and their scientific advisors that British beef was safe for consumption (Gregory, 2001).

Since the mid-1980s, the efforts to enhance public understanding of science have relied on a broad range of grassroots and out-reach activities (House of Lords, 2000). These have included competitions for children across the various scientific societies, increasing the availability of interactive experimental exhibits in museums, and providing opportunities for exchange between schools, Higher Education and industry (e.g. The Royal Society, 1985). The efforts taken to enhance public understanding of science have been concerted, multifaceted, and have helped to dissolve the barriers between scientists and the public, and between scientists and the media. Importantly, the focus on out-reach activities has replaced a paternalistic or condescending top-down approach to 'educating' the public in science matters (House of Lords, 2000; Gregory, 2001).

In their discussions about enhancing public understanding of climate change in the USA, Nisbet (2009) and Nisbet and Kotcher (2009) stress the importance of recruiting influential peers at grassroots level. Influential peers do not necessarily require expertise or to hold positions of power. Instead, they are 'information brokers' (Nisbet & Kotcher, 2009), who pass on information to their peers, co-workers, family, friends or social group. Campbell *et al.* (2008) discuss the effectiveness of influential peers in an experimental study in which school children were recruited to discourage the take up of smoking among their classmates during informal out-of-class interactions. Similarly, with approximately 5 million visits per month, the parents using the website mumsnet.com represent a large community of influential peers. The website members have been effective in sharing information among parents in the UK and organising campaigns relating to education, child welfare and other parenting issues (see website for details).

An influential peer approach may gain support among teachers. Chamberlain (2012a) found that teachers believed that any efforts to improve understanding of assessment should be filtered through teachers to students and parents, rather than focusing on the public more generally. Influential peers could also be recruited among students, school and college examination officers, parents, Parent and Teacher Associations, school and college governors or trustees, providers of teacher training, and learner support groups or organisations. With a diverse range of influential peers, this approach could increase the likelihood that important messages about assessment reach individuals from a diverse range of socio-educational groups. Ofqual has conducted a series of assessment-related workshops at events including the UK Youth Parliament Annual Conference and the National Learner Panel (Opposs & He, 2012b). Similar events may be a first step in increasing interaction with qualification users and gaining support for an influential peer approach.

Qualification awarding bodies tend to have limited contact with qualification users, with teachers and examinations officers usually the main points of contact. There are few access points through which qualification awarding bodies can interact with the users of the qualifications they offer, and relations therefore tend to be institutional and 'faceless' (Giddens, 1990). Further, the templates used in the production of news media most closely fit 'bad news stories' of technical or human errors in the assessment system and the 'falling standards' frame (Warmington & Murphy, 2007). It appears unlikely, then, that pursuing increased media coverage may overcome or counteract the lack of access points and negative reporting to generate the outcomes desired by Ofqual and educational assessors. An influential peer approach, based on interpersonal relations and face-to-face interaction that is driven by the qualification users themselves, therefore, may be more fruitful.

Concluding comments

This paper has drawn upon experiences in other fields that attract considerable public interest, sometimes in controversial circumstances, but not always a widely assimilated understanding of their technical and factual dimensions. These fields offer ideas for three communication strategies that could be applied to assessment information: presenting information in frames, focusing on the application of assessment information, and recruiting influential peers as information brokers. The recommendations may stimulate critical debate about their potential utility, or may trigger other proposals. As such, this paper has not been concerned to address practical matters such as how to develop frames, recruit influential peers, ensure out-reach to diverse socio-educational groups, or explore who among the assessment community is best placed to offer leadership for such actions. Any approach to communication requires careful thought and piloting to avoid under-mining public confidence, especially the confidence of the primary qualification users: students and teachers. The experiences of scientists in improving public understanding of science in the UK demonstrate that there may be many more approaches, such as various out-reach activities, that educational assessors may consider using. The experiences of scientists also suggest that improving public understanding requires sustained effort over many years.

Assessment specialists may question the appropriateness of presenting complex statistical or conceptual information in simplified frames, or of conferring the responsibility for dissemination to influential peers. Both options appear to argue the case for decreasing the visibility of educational assessors and de-emphasising their specialist knowledge. In addition, by adopting the approaches outlined in this paper, it is possible that qualification users would receive only partial information. There is a delicate balance to be struck between presenting sufficient information to be informative, and providing a level of detail that has the potential to alienate the intended audiences. Arguably, a partial understanding is at least a starting point for achieving the goal of enhancing public understanding of assessment. Moreover, if the public's interest was stimulated, resources could be provided for those who wish to follow up the various concerns in greater depth.

Educational assessment is a specialist, technical field. Compared with science, it may not be perceived as interesting or relevant to the general public. However, it is undoubtedly of significant relevance to those who are currently studying, teaching or using the qualifications of the national assessment system. Ofqual and others have identified the need to communicate, or to communicate better, about a range of assessment matters. Educational assessment, as a discipline, is seemingly lagging behind other disciplines in terms of implementing strategies to enhance communication and understanding of its key dimensions. However, this means that educational assessors are well placed to take advantage of the lessons learnt across other disciplines.

Note

1. AQA: http://www.aqa.org.uk; Edexcel: http://www.edexcel.com/Pages/Home.aspx; Oxford Cambridge and RSA Examinations: http://www.ocr.org.uk/index.html

References

American Educational Research Association, American Psychological Association, National Council on Measurement in Education (1999). *Standards for educational and psychological testing*. Washington, American Educational Research Association.

Baird, J., Béguin, A., Black, P., Pollitt, A. & Stanley, G. (2012). The reliability programme: final report of the technical advisory group, in: D. Opposs & Q. He (Eds) *Ofqual's reliability compendium*. Coventry, Office of Qualifications and Examinations Regulation, 771–838.

Becker, D.E., Wise, L.L., Hardoin, M.M. & Watters, C. (Eds) (2011). *Independent evaluation of the California High School Exit Examination: 2011 evaluation report*. Virginia, Human Resources Research Organisation.

Bellaby, P. (2003). Communication and miscommunication of risk: understanding UK parents' attitudes to combined MMR vaccination. *British Medical Journal*, 327, 725–728.

Betebenner, D., Shang, Y., Xiang, Y., Zhao, Y. & Yue, X. (2008). The impact of performance level misclassification on the accuracy and precision of percent at performance level measures. *Journal of Educational Measurement*, 45(2), 119–137.

Boyle, A., Opposs, D. & Kinsella, A. (2012). No news is good news? Talking to the public about the reliability of assessment, in: D. Opposs & Q. He (Eds) *Ofqual's reliability compendium*. Coventry, Office of Qualifications and Examinations Regulation, 653–664.

Bramley, T. & Dhawan, V. (2012). Estimates of reliability of qualifications, in: D. Opposs & Q. He (Eds) *Ofqual's reliability compendium*. Coventry, Office of Qualifications and Examinations Regulation, 217–319.

Burkeman, O. (2003, 4 March). Memo exposes Bush's new green strategy. *The Guardian*.

Burslem, S. (2012). The reliability programme: final report of the policy advisory group, in: D. Opposs & Q. He (Eds) *Ofqual's reliability compendium*. Coventry, Office of Qualifications and Examinations Regulation, 839–851.

Campbell, R., Starkey, F., Holliday, J., Audrey, S., Bloor, M., Parry-Langdon, N., Hughes, R. & Moore, L. (2008). An informal school-based peer-led intervention for smoking prevention in adolescence (ASSIST): a cluster randomised trial. *Lancet*, 371, 1595–1602.

Chamberlain, S. (2012a). Public perceptions of reliability, in: D. Opposs & Q. He (Eds) *Ofqual's reliability compendium*. Coventry, Office of Qualifications and Examinations Regulation, 691–725.

Chamberlain, S. (2012b). 'Maybe I'm not as good as I think I am'. How qualification users interpret their examination results, *Educational Research*, 54(1), 39–49.

Dale, G. (2008). 'Green shift': an analysis of corporate responses to climate change. *International Journal of Management Concepts and Philosophy*, 3(2), 134–155.

Department of Energy and Climate Change (2012) News: the Clean Energy Ministerial. Available online at: http://www.decc.gov.uk/en/content/cms/news/cem3/cem3.aspx (accessed 5 April 2012).

Fisher, K. (1997). Locating frames in the discursive universe. *Sociological Research Online*, 2(3). Available online at: http://www.socresonline.org.uk/2/3/4.html (accessed 5 April 2012).

Giddens, A. (1990). *The consequences of modernity*. Cambridge, Polity Press.

Goodman, D.P. & Hambleton, R.K. (2004). Student test score reports and interpretive guides: review of current practices and suggestions for future research. *Applied Measurement in Education*, 17(2), 145–220.

Gregory, J. (2001). Public understanding of science: lessons from the UK experience. *Science and Development Network*. Available online at: http://www.scidev.net/en/features/public-understanding-of-science-lessons-from the.html (accessed 20 February 2012).

Harlen, W. (1994). Developing public understanding of education: a role for educational researchers. *British Educational Research Journal*, 20(1), 3–16.

Hattie, J. (May, 2010). Visibly learning from reports: the validity of score reports. *Online Educational Research Journal*. Available online at: http://www.oerj.org/View?action=view-PDF&paper=6 (accessed 30 January 2012).

He, Q., Opposs, D. & Boyle, A. (2012). A quantitative investigation into public perceptions of reliability in examination results in England, in: D. Opposs & Q. He (Eds) *Ofqual's reliability compendium*. Coventry, Office of Qualifications and Examinations Regulation, 727–767.

House of Lords (2000). *Science and technology—third report*. Available online at: http://www.publications.parliament.uk/pa/ld199900/ldselect/ldsctech/38/3801.htm (accessed 5 February 2012).

Johnson, S. & Johnson, R. (2012). Conceptualising and interpreting reliability, in: D. Opposs & Q. He (Eds) *Ofqual's reliability compendium*. Coventry, Office of Qualifications and Examinations Regulation, 459–521.

Johnson, F., Burrough, N., Ziff, A. & Collins, B. (2012). Public perceptions of reliability in examinations, in: D. Opposs & Q. He (Eds) *Ofqual's reliability compendium*. Coventry, Office of Qualifications and Examinations Regulation, 667–689.

Murphy, R. (2004). *Grades of uncertainty. Reviewing the uses and misuses of examination grades*. London, Association of Teachers and Lecturers.

Newton, P.E. (2005). The public understanding of measurement inaccuracy. *British Educational Research Journal*, 31(4), 419–442.

Newton, P.E. (2007). Clarifying the purposes of educational assessment. *Assessment in Education: Principles, Policy & Practice*, 14(2), 149–170.

Nisbet, M.C. (2009). Communicating climate change: why frames matter for public engagement. *Environment: Science and Policy for Sustainable Development*, 51(2), 12–23.

Nisbet, M.C. & Kotcher, J. (2009). A two-step flow of influence? Opinion-leader campaigns on climate change. *Science Communication* 30(3), 328–354.

Nordhaus, T. & Schellenberger, M. (2007). *Break through: from the death of environmentalism to the politics of possibility*. New York, NY, Houghton Mifflin.

Office of Qualifications and Examinations Regulation (2009). *What is Ofqual's reliability programme?* Coventry, Office of Qualifications and Examinations Regulation.

Office of Qualifications and Examinations Regulation (2012). *The assessment validity programme.* Available online at: http://www.ofqual.gov.uk/standards/validity/ (accessed online 11 April 2012).

Offit, P.A. & Coffin, S.E. (2003). Communicating science to the public: MMR vaccine and autism. *Vaccine*, 22, 1–6.

O'Neill, O. (2002). *A question of trust: the BBC Reith Lectures 2002.* Cambridge, Cambridge University Press.

Opposs, D. & He, Q. (Eds) (2012a). *Ofqual's reliability compendium.* Coventry, Office of Qualifications and Examinations Regulation.

Opposs, D. & He, Q. (2012b). The reliability programme: final report, in: D. Opposs & Q. He (Eds) *Ofqual's reliability compendium.* Coventry, Office of Qualifications and Examinations Regulation, 853–898.

Petts, J. & Niemeyer, S. (2004). Health risk communication and amplification: learning from the MMR vaccination controversy. *Health, Risk & Society*, 6(1), 7–23.

Phelps, R.P., Zenisky, A., Hambleton, R.K. & Sireci, S.G. (2012). On the reporting of measurement uncertainty and reliability for U.S. Educational and Licensure Tests, in: D. Opposs & Q. He (Eds) *Ofqual's reliability compendium.* Coventry, Office of Qualifications and Examinations Regulation, 605–641.

Riesch, H. & Spiegelhalter, D. (2011). 'Careless pork costs lives': risk stories from science to press release to media. *Health, Risk & Society*, 13(1), 47–64.

The Royal Society (1985). *The public understanding of science.* London, The Royal Society.

Salvagno, M. & Teglasi, H. (1987). Teacher perceptions of different types of information in psychological reports. *Journal of School Psychology*, 25, 415–424.

Tufte, E. R. (2001). *The visual display of quantitative information* (2nd edn.). Connecticut, Graphics Press.

Wakefield, A.J., Murch, S.H., Anthony, A., Linnell, J., Casson, D.M., Malik, M., *et al.* (1998). Ileal-lymphoid-nodular hyperplasia, non-specific colitis, and pervasive developmental disorder in children. *Lancet*, 351, 637–641.

Warmington, P. & Murphy, R. (2004). Could do better? Media depictions of UK educational assessment results. *Journal of Education Policy*, 19(3), 285–299.

Warmington, P. & Murphy, R. (2007). 'Read all about it!' UK news media coverage of A-level results. *Policy Futures in Education*, 5(1), 70–83.

Wheadon, C. & Stockford, I. (2012). Classification accuracy and consistency in GCSE and A-level examinations offered by the Assessment and Qualifications Alliance (AQA) November 2008 to June 2009. in: D. Opposs & Q. He (Eds) *Ofqual's reliability compendium.* Coventry, Office of Qualifications and Examinations Regulation, 107–139.

Wheadon, C., Whitehouse, C., Spalding, V., Tremain, K. & Charman, M. (2009). *Principles and practice of on-demand testing.* Coventry, Office of Qualifications and Examinations Regulation.

Misleading the public understanding of assessment: wilful or wrongful interpretation by government and media

Warwick Mansell

London, UK

This paper considers the public debate surrounding assessment in English education and presents evidence of the misuse of public data from national tests. Statistics generated by pupil assessments in schools and colleges in England are argued to be subject to misinterpretation by the media and policy makers. The discourse tends either to be sensationalist—for example, raising public anxiety by claiming falling standards—or politically charged—for example, where the incumbent government is criticised by its political enemies for pursuing failing policies—rather than being framed by objective and purposeful interpretations. Examples are provided to illustrate how interpretations by the media and policy-makers can be strikingly at odds with how the figures should properly be read. The paper analyses the propriety of these interpretations and makes suggestions as to how a more cautious approach to the use of results in the public sphere can be promoted.

Introduction

Over the past two decades, UK national assessment policy and its outcomes in various contexts, for example National Curriculum tests, and General Certificate of Secondary Education (GCSE) and Advanced-level General Certificate of Education (A-level) qualifications, have attracted political and media criticism on almost an annual basis corresponding to the publication of the relevant results. It is the contention of this paper that much of this criticism arises from the misuse and/or misinterpretation of assessment data, some of it wilful in pursuit of political ends, some of it the result of a superficial treatment of the data that is designed to provoke sensational headlines. These are bold statements and as the paper proceeds they will be supported with evidence that draws on examples from policy and media contexts. However, misuse and misinterpretation of data are potentially overlapping processes and even specific instances can be complexly nuanced. To keep the analysis manageable, therefore, two categories are used to frame the paper, namely:

- Media and policy-related misuse of published results
- Misuse of data in policy formulation and implementation.

Media and policy-related misuse of results

Sections of the media in the UK, as in most democratic countries, are often given to a degree of hyperbole, with a propensity to produce headlines that are more eye-catching and alarming than a more cautious reading of the facts might suggest. In the context of school examination results in England (and to a lesser extent in the three other countries of the UK: Wales, Northern Ireland and Scotland), the lack of an evidence base for some claims, which have featured prominently in press coverage and have the potential to shape public perceptions of what is going on in schools, is on occasion striking. In England, the frequent targets for criticism are the assessments associated with the National Curriculum, and particularly those at Key Stage 2, which is the final stage of schooling in primary schools (children aged approximately 7–11 years).

For example, In May 2011, London's *Evening Standard* newspaper launched a prominent and seemingly influential campaign to improve reading standards in the city by including in its front page the 'shocking' claim that 'One in four children is "practically illiterate" on leaving primary school', i.e. at the end of Key Stage 2. This was included in the article's second paragraph, under a headline which said: 'A city of children who cannot read' (*London Evening Standard*, 2011). Inside, the news article softened its 'illiterate' claim to: 'One in four children leaves the capital's state primaries [primary schools] unable to read properly'. Yet close inspection of the figures used, and their interpretation, shows that they were clearly at odds with the published Key Stage 2 results in at least two aspects: the use of the term 'practically illiterate' and the quoted proportions relating to it.

The first departure of the quoted statistics from the official data was that the latter showed that some 85% of pupils in England achieved government expectations of a Level 4 or higher in reading tests in 2010, the last year for which the *Evening Standard* would have had figures at the time of the coverage (DfE, 2010a). National Curriculum Key Stage 2 tests are marked against a set of attainment targets and pupil performance is recorded in 'levels', which are set out in the current version of the primary National Curriculum, established in 1999 (QCA, 1999; QCDA, 2010). Level 4 in reading is defined as:

In responding to a range of texts, pupils show understanding of significant ideas, themes, events and characters, beginning to use inference and deduction. They refer to the text when explaining their views. They locate and use ideas and information. (QCDA, 2010, p. 17)

In the year in question, industrial action relating to the burden and purpose of the tests resulted in almost 4000 primary schools boycotting the Key Stage 2 national tests, which has the potential to undermine the argument that the data reflect the results from all schools. However, the government publication releasing the results states clearly that 'The Department head of professional statistics has determined that a sufficient volume of results is available to give a representative estimate of achievement nationally' (DfE, 2010b). Therefore the official data support the view that only 15% of pupils had not achieved Level 4 in the tests.

Clearly, then, if one accepts the information from these tests, it is not true that 25% of London pupils were 'practically illiterate', as claimed on the front page, or 'cannot read', as claimed in the headline, unless London can be shown to have an achievement profile dramatically lower than the nationally determined proportion of at least 85% meeting the definition above, which manifestly does not reflect illiteracy. In addition, the official statistics show that, in England as a whole, a further 8% of pupils achieved Level 3 in the reading tests (DfE, 2010a). This level is defined as pupils being able to 'read a range of texts fluently and accurately'. Not only is this a significantly higher level of competence than 'illiterate', it also means that 93% (85+8) of pupils that year were given Level 3 or above in the tests and by definition could 'read fluently'. A further 1% of pupils in schools doing the tests did not sit them, leading to the conclusion that only 6% can safely be assumed to have achieved a performance below Level 3. The question is begged: how did the *Evening Standard* arrive at its conclusion that 25% of pupils were leaving London primary schools 'practically illiterate'?

The headline 'one in four practically illiterate' was clearly misleading and even mischievous. One group, Full Fact (2011), probed the provenance of the figures and the *Evening Standard* directed them to a report on literacy, commissioned from the think tank, the Centre for Policy Studies, by the mayor of London, Boris Johnson. This report, which itself had gained national media coverage on the BBC's website (BBC, 2010a) and in the *Daily Express* newspaper (*Daily Express*, 2010) quotes a figure of a third, rather than a quarter, of pupils leaving London primary schools as having difficulties with reading, but includes no reference for the source of this figure. When Full Fact requested the sources for this, it was told that two sources were used. The first was another think tank report, this time the Policy Exchange (Richmond & Freedman, 2009), which had relied on National Curriculum test data. The other was information gathered from just two secondary academy schools on the reading standards of pupils joining them from primary schools. So, despite the problems behind this statistic—it appears either to be a serious and basic misinterpretation of official data or to be based on a very small sample—the 25% figure became the centrepiece for the *Evening Standard*'s launch of a campaign to get more of the capital's children reading.

Some will argue that the worthiness of such a campaign makes any statistical misinterpretation or misuse less important, but this stance ignores the fact that however noble any implication might be, the misuse of statistics also has negative ramifications. For example, parents might lose confidence in schools as a result of being misled about what is known about reading standards. And when such misuse is sustained as credible in subsequent debates, the damaging effect on education is compounded. For example, the 'one in four' figure in relation to London's schools was repeated almost a year later in an article quoting the London mayor, which led the front page of the *Guardian* newspaper in March, 2012 (Wintour & Mulholland, 2012). The article reported that the mayor of London, Boris Johnson, was seeking greater influence over education in the capital and was claiming that 'poor schooling', including young people leaving school unable to read properly, contributed to the notorious August 2011 riots in London and other English cities. He was quoted as saying: 'There are too many people who feel there is no future for them in this city. I want to try to deal with these kids at an earlier age and trying to crack illiteracy—that is at the heart of this. It is crucial that we invest in literacy ...'. In seven London boroughs there '... are one in four kids reaching the age of 11 who are unable to read properly. That is the best place to start.' At the time I asked the mayor's office for further information on the statistics quoted but no reply was received.

Staying on the subject of enquiries into the causes of the riots of August 2011, a press release issued by the Riots Communities and Victims Panel, a committee which was set up by the government following the disturbances, included the following statement:

> Children are leaving school unable to read and write—one fifth of school leavers have the literacy skills of an eleven year old, or younger. (Riots Communities and Victims Panel, 2012)

Again, this incorrectly asserts that young people, who have achieved the government expectation for 11-year-olds, i.e. Level 4 in reading and writing, cannot read and write. The definition for Level 4 reading above clearly contests such an interpretation and Level 4 in writing equally dispels the notion of illiteracy: 'Pupils' writing in a range of forms is lively and thoughtful ... Handwriting style is fluent, joined and legible' (QCDA, 2010, p. 18).

Clearly, if a young person is leaving school 'with the literacy skills of an 11-year-old', it does not mean they are unable to read and write. A simple check of the definitions of the assessment information underlying these statistical claims would have made this clear, and an assessment expert would have been able to point out how the statement as it stands is misleading and inaccurate.

Another example in this category relates to coverage of literacy statistics on the BBC's Radio 4 *Today* programme on 17 December 2010. This analysed Key Stage 2 test data from the same year as discussed above—2010—and reported that 10% of 11-year-old boys in England 'reached the reading standards of seven-year-olds or below'. Following an interview with the Education Secretary, Michael Gove, this led to a headline on the programme's website saying: 'Gove: 11-year-old illiteracy 'unacceptable'' (BBC, 2010b). Gove's interviewer also used the term 'illiteracy', during the discussion with the Education Secretary.

This is another demonstrably incorrect and misleading misinterpretation. The programme based its discussion on the percentage of 11-year-old boys, taking Key Stage 2 reading tests, who had been graded at Level 2 or below. Since Level 2 is the government's 'expected' level for seven-year-olds, this 10% of boys were said to have the reading age of seven-year-olds. This, then, seemed to be the programme's definition of 'illiteracy'. However, Level 2 recognises 'reading of simple texts [that] shows understanding and is generally accurate' (QCDA, 2010, p. 17). Achieving the government's 'expected' Level 2 in reading tests cannot therefore be termed 'illiterate'. It may be argued that the percentage of pupils performing at this lower-than-expected level for their age is a worrying fact, but it is mischievous to describe it as 'illiterate'. It is even more puzzling because the official data (DfE, 2010c) do not record any boys with Level 2. Instead the figures show that 6% of pupils were not entered for the tests because they were believed by their teacher not to be likely to gain a level, while a further 4% took the tests but did not achieve a level. The combination of these appears to have accounted for the 10% of boys 'achieving at Level 2 or below'.

One obvious weakness in the programme's treatment of the matter was that it did not mention the error margins that have been shown to exist around any National Curriculum test results (for a discussion about communicating the reliability of test scores to the public, see Boyle *et al.*, 2009). As mentioned above, the 4% of pupils failing to achieve Level 3 in the one-off reading comprehension test may have over or under-performed on the day; or there could have been errors in the marking. The programme also failed to point out that very small differences in the performance of pupils on this test could lead to very large differences in interpretation. For example, at 10 marks out of 50, an 11-year-old pupil would be deemed to have achieved just below the threshold for Level 3 (11 marks) while a pupil with a score of 18 would achieve Level 4 (for threshold scores, see DfE, 2012c).

According to the programme's interpretation, then, the former pupil would 'have the reading age of a seven-year-old' whilst the latter would be performing at the government's expected level for 11-year-olds. Listeners were not told that as few as eight marks distinguished the possible scores for pupils below Level 3 and at Level 4, and could be forgiven for assuming that a large proportion of 11-year-old boys were four years behind with their reading. Taking this interpretation at face value, a seven-year-old taking this test and achieving the government expectation for their age, and then sitting a similar one again when aged 11, would be deemed to have made four years' progress if they advanced by eight marks over this period, or two marks per academic year. In other words, four years' difference in the expected reading age can actually come down to just eight marks on a one-off test. Worse still, the four years notionally between Level 3 and Level 4 could be characterised by a score difference of just one mark, at the threshold of 17 marks for the award of Level 3 and 18 marks gaining a Level 4. The presenters of the *Today* programme did not take these issues into account and inappropriately linked the results to a national level of 'illiteracy'. They asserted, without further investigation or scepticism, that those not reaching Level 3 had the reading age expected of a seven-year-old. The damage that these otherwise highly respected commentators do to public understanding of assessment results is difficult to assess but could be significant.

This example demonstrates that the media interpretation of literacy statistics can be particularly problematic. However, they are not the only sphere of public debate in which assessment information can be misused, or at least not presented in a way that gives the public an objective sense of how statistical data are being interpreted. For example, newspapers and broadcasters take considerable interest in the government's benchmark indicator for national performance in General Certificate of Secondary Education examinations (GCSEs). They often quote comparative figures for the proportion of English, Welsh and Northern Ireland pupils achieving five A*–C grades (including English and mathematics), with the proportion for 2011 in England being 59% (DfE, 2012a).

C grades can be the threshold qualifications in English and mathematics for many employment opportunities or further education, so perhaps unsurprisingly, the 40% or so not achieving at least a C grade often prompts the media to couch this statistic in a negative sense, perhaps quoting it with the qualifier 'only'. However, the reporting frequently gives little sense, or an incomplete sense, of the trends in results over a period of time. For example, by 2010 the number of pupils achieving the government target had risen by more than 50% since 1996, while in 2011 results on this benchmark indicator jumped by their greatest margin since the government began recording the figures in 1996 (DfE, 2011; DfE, 2012b). Media coverage, including pieces in the *Daily Telegraph* (Paton, 2011) and on the BBC website (Harrison, 2011), gave little sense of this change. The 2012 furore over the fall in GCSE passes at A*–C (see for example the article in the *Daily Telegraph*, 2012) was paradoxically fuelled by media coverage that centred on alleged manipulation of the results by examination boards and the regulator, Ofqual.

Misuse of data in policy formulation and implementation

The previous examples demonstrate how data relating to national assessments can be misinterpreted or misrepresented. Under the second category of misuse of assessment data, consideration is now given to the extent to which such data are manipulated in policy-making and policy implementation contexts. One example involves the use by the former Labour government of a graphical representation purporting to illustrate how pupils progress—or not—through National Curriculum levels. In 2006, the Department for Education and Skills hosted a briefing on national test results, presented by the Labour government's chief advisor for school standards, Sue Hackman. A chart in the presentation depicted 100 'stickmen', each of which represented 1% of pupils nationally. The graphic became very popular and featured in a video first aired on Teachers TV (2006). One version of the graphic compared pupils' results at Key Stage 2 and in the, now defunct, Key Stage 3 tests. Its argued virtues included the facility to reconfigure it to work at the local authority level or at the school level, depending on which set of results was being analysed. The inferences drawn from the comparison proved to be exceptionally simplistic, and therefore problematic.

The nub of the argument was that the graph showed how pupils with the same levels at Key Stage 3 as they had achieved at Key Stage 2 were 'stuck', having apparently made no progress over the intervening three years. In the Teachers TV interview mentioned above (Teachers TV, 2006), Hackman identified six 'stickmen', i.e. 6% of pupils, who were in this position nationally. She said: 'We have 6% who are stuck at Level 4: they left primary school at national expectations [i.e. Level 4] and then sat for three years in secondary school and did not add a single level'. But a number of obvious questions immediately suggest themselves. For example, what if the pupils in question had simply over or under-performed on either test occasion? Does this analysis take into account the possibility of marking error? Did the two tests sample different parts of the English curriculum, on one of which the pupils were strong, and on the other they were weak? Perhaps more fundamentally, did a judgement of a particular level at Key Stage 3 mean the same thing—in terms of its relationship to underlying understanding and mastery of this subject—as it did at Key Stage 2? The answers to such questions would probably render the 'no progress' verdicts very dubious.

One aspect of the Teachers TV presentation was a discussion on how the graphic could be used in individual schools and how it might prompt schools to take different teaching approaches with different pupils. The need for an acknowledgement of error margins and limitations around the data should have been obvious, and flagged up for the teacher audience, especially if—worryingly—teaching strategies pursued with individual children could change depending on the information provided in these charts. The notion of an individual child receiving a 'no progress' message when in fact one or both test judgements had been subject to error would be particularly worrying. Yet this interpretative approach has been widely promoted by the government (see for example DCSF, 2008).

Policy proposals that fail to take sufficient account of whether assessment-generated statistics are suited for the task for which they are being put forward form another aspect of this category of misuse. Take, for example, a paper published in 2011 by the charity, the Sutton Trust (2011), which advocated greater use of performance-related pay for teachers. Two components of the process were proposed to include 'value-added' test or examination results and a personal evaluation by the teachers' line manager, the headteacher, which also includes a test result related element. The rationale put forward by the paper was that headteachers '... could be incentivised into rewarding high-performing teachers by relating their pay to overall test score gains made by their pupils'. Another example in the same vein is the proposal made by Allen and Burgess (2012) to create a new system for deciding which teachers should be allowed to pursue a long-term career in the profession. They suggest that initial teacher education providers should adopt a more relaxed attitude to the recruitment of teachers on to their courses, but that stricter selection criteria should be applied part-way into the teachers' careers, with only the 'most effective' being allowed to continue into a classroom career. They propose that after a period of perhaps three years, 'measures of teacher effectiveness in facilitating pupil progress' should be used to judge who should be allowed to continue in their careers and who should not. Although they concede that '... estimates of teacher effectiveness will never be perfect, and a good deal of evidence over a number of years will be necessary to reach a decision' they argue that such an approach '... is clearly necessary to raise the average effectiveness of the teaching profession in England'.

Pupils' test and examination results are the basis for the measures in these two sets of proposals, but are they suited for such a purpose? Do they in any way measure what is considered to be good quality teaching, or are they being used simply because they reflect an aspect of the outcome of teaching that is easier than other aspects to measure? What is the scope for error in individual test data, and in the final judgements on teacher quality? Is it possible to capture the effects of an individual teacher on pupil achievement in any test, or should each teacher be seen only as building on the efforts of others? Perhaps most importantly, what would be the effect on teachers' behaviour if such measures were to be introduced? For example, would it encourage teachers to narrow their teaching priorities to focus excessively on ensuring they did well on these measures? Allen (2012) make no attempt to address such issues and the Sutton Trust paper only briefly raises the question of 'validity, stability and precision' (Sutton Trust, 2011, nn. 29, 30).

Concluding remarks

At the outset of this paper, I suggested that there were at least two broad categories of misuse of assessment data by the media and policy-makers. The examples presented illustrate how some of these arise and how they may be wilfully promoted or naively misinterpreted, resulting in sensationalist outputs or political point-scoring. Whether wilful manipulation or naïve misinterpretation, I would argue that a considerable reduction in their incidence and impact could be effected if two remedies were applied. First, as argued elsewhere in this special issue, there is a need to communicate the possibility of measurement error in assessment results to a wider audience. Ignoring the possibility of measurement error is only one type of possible misinterpretation of results in the media and by policy-makers; its dangers are perhaps best illustrated in the 'stickmen' example above. However, being more open about the limits on the degree of certainty behind assessment statistics would make a considerable contribution to the public debate. It is not an easy remedy but a number of recent studies have sought to quantify the uncertainty around National Curriculum test level judgements for individual children (Ofqual, 2011). Consideration should be given to publishing error margins around individual test judgements. 'Health warnings' around school-by-school statistics should emphasise that they can provide only a partial appraisal of the quality of education that goes on in each institution, and that they are often significantly influenced by factors beyond a school's control (for example, see Mansell *et al.*, 2009).

Second, and perhaps more fundamentally, assessment experts need to engage more fully with public discussions relating to assessment information, and must speak out if they feel such information is being misused or misinterpreted. For several years now, I have worked in the space between the assessment community, on the one hand, and the mainstream media, on the other. Given the wealth of knowledge and technical expertise which exists in the former, and the appetite for assessment-related news in the latter, it is surprising in my view that there is not greater interaction between the two. With assessment data now right at the heart of questions about whether schools are succeeding or failing to educate young people effectively, the need for such engagement is pressing.

References

Allen, R. & Burgess, S. (2012). Reforming teacher training. Centre for Market and Public Organisation blog. Available online at: http://cmpo.wordpress.com/2012/05/03/reforming-teacher-training/

BBC (2010a). 'Third' of London primary pupils have reading problems. British Broadcasting Corporation. Available online at: http://www.bbc.co.uk/news/uk-england-london-10686477

BBC (2010b). Radio 4 *Today* programme: Gove: Eleven-year-old illiteracy 'unacceptable'. British Broadcasting Corporation, Available online at: http://news.bbc.co.uk/today/hi/today/newsid_9297000/9297191.stm

Boyle, A., Opposs, D. & Kinsella, A. (2009). No news is good news: talking to the public about the reliability of assessment. Paper presented at the *35th International Assessment for Educational Assessment (IAEA) annual conference*, Brisbane, Australia, 13–18 September.

Daily Express (2010). Education: a third of pupils are still unable to read aged 11. Available online at: http://www.express.co.uk/posts/view/187732/Education-A-third-of-pupils-are-still-unable-to-read-aged-11

Daily Telegraph (2012). GCSE results: more students to appeal over 'manipulated' grades. Available online at: http://www.telegraph.co.uk/education/secondaryeducation/9495370/GCSE-results-more-students-to-appeal-over-manipulated-grades.html

DCSF (2008). Making good progress in Key Stage 3 English. Department for Children, Schools and Families. Available online at: http://www.educationnorth.co.uk/docs/DCSF_KS3_English.pdf

DfE (2010a). National Curriculum assessments at Key Stage 2 in England 2009/10 (revised). Department for Education. Available online at: http://www.education.gov.uk/rsgateway/DB/SFR/s000975/index.shtml (Table 8 of the first Excel spreadsheet) (accessed 19 May 2012).

DfE (2010b). National Curriculum assessments at Key Stage 2 in England 2009/10 (revised) pdf version. Department for Education. Available online at: http://www.education.gov.uk/rsgateway/DB/SFR/s000975/sfr36-2010.pdf (accessed 19 May 2012).

DfE (2010c). National Curriculum Assessments at Key Stage 2 in England 2009/10 (revised) Department for Education. Available online at: http://www.education.gov.uk/rsgateway/DB/SFR/s000975/index.shtml (Table 3 of first Excel spreadsheet) (accessed 19 May 2012).

DfE (2011). GCSE and equivalent results in England, 2010/11 (Provisional). Department for Education Available online at: http://www.education.gov.uk/rsgateway/DB/SFR/s001034/index.shtml (Table 1a) (accessed 16 July 2012).

DfE (2012a). GCSE and equivalent results in England, 2010/11 (revised). Department for Education. Available online at: http://www.education.gov.uk/rsgateway/DB/SFR/s001056/index.shtml (accessed 16 July 2012).

DfE (2012b). GCSE and equivalent results in England, 2010/11 (revised). Department for Education. Available online at: http://www.education.gov.uk/rsgateway/DB/SFR/s001056/index.shtml (Table 1a) (accessed 16 July 2012).

DfE (2012c). Threshold tables and standardised scores: level threshold scores. Department for Education. Available online at: http://www.education.gov.uk/schools/teachingandlearning/assessment/keystage2/pupil/b00206193/ks2-results/level-threshold-tables

Full Fact (2011). Literacy in London: PCC judgement sheds no light on school standards. Available online at: http://fullfact.org/blog/London_schools_literacy_children_PCC-3192 (accessed 18 May 2012).

Harrison, A. (2011). Rise in pupils getting five good GCSEs including English and maths. BBC News website. Available online at: http://www.bbc.co.uk/news/education-15383548

London Evening Standard (2011). A city of children who cannot read. Available online at: http://www.thisislondon.co.uk/news/a-city-of-children-who-cannot-read-6406797.html

Mansell, W., James, M. & the Assessment Reform Group (2009). Assessment in schools: fit for purpose? A commentary by the Teaching and Learning Research Programme. Available online at: http://www.tlrp.org/pub/documents/assessment.pdf

Ofqual (2011). The reliability programme: final report of the technical advisory group. Available online at: https://docs.google.com/viewer?a=v&q=cache:vCqhH3kTuQsJ:www2.ofqual.gov.uk/downloads/category/193-reliability-compendium%3Fdownload%3D1271%253Athe-reliability-programme-final-report-of-the-technical-advisory-group-march-2011+&hl=en&gl=uk&pid=bl&srcid=ADGEESjAEGyVXRlTL4X1YaLfItnN0WOo3hXUs0yJ5MXtAfFqJcxn5_CQ_VpnoopBX6MXdtHOt5lRpoDahsWmXHMr_vTx8iEBDqd3B9h9W6pqStKAWM3D1TIzsDEH_81x-GEvf9NcHzXM&sig=AHIEtbQbMLRnKlrh3vE6Wwg7BZWJWzQtuw

Paton, G. (2011). GCSE results: teenagers failing to study tough subjects. Daily Telegraph. Available online at: http://www.telegraph.co.uk/education/educationnews/8838748/GCSE-results-teenagers-failing-to-study-tough-subjects.html

QCA(1999). The National Curriculum: handbook for primary teachers in England: Key Stages 1 and 2. See Qualifications and Curriculum Authority. Available online at: https://www.education.gov.uk/publications/eOrderingDownload/QCA-99-457.pdf

QCDA (2010). The National Curriculum: level descriptions for subjects. See Qualifications and Curriculum Development Agency. Available online at: http://dera.ioe.ac.uk/10747/1/1849623848.pdf

Richmond, T. & Freedman, S. (2009). Rising marks, falling standards: an investigation into literacy, numeracy and science in primary and secondary schools. Policy Exchange. Available online at: http://www.policyexchange.org.uk/images/publications/rising%20marks%20falling %20standards%20-%20apr%2009.pdf

Riots Communities and Victims Panel (2012). Riots Communities and Victims Panel publishes final report. Available online at: http://riotspanel.independent.gov.uk/news/riots-communities-and-victims-panel-publishes-final-report/

Sutton Trust (2011). Improving the impact of teachers on pupil achievement in the UK—interim findings. Available online at: http://www.suttontrust.com/public/documents/ 1teachers-impact-report-final.pdf

Teachers TV (2006). Personalising progress. Available online at: http://www.playbackschools. org.uk/programme/3038/personalising-progress (accessed 16 July 2012).

Wintour, P. & Mulholland, H. (2012). Boris Johnson says poor schools helped cause riots. *Guardian*. Available online at: http://www.guardian.co.uk/politics/2012/mar/23/boris-johnson-bad-schools-london-riots

Media roles in influencing the public understanding of educational assessment issues

Roger Murphy

University of Nottingham, UK

This paper explores the media coverage of UK national examination results. Utilising the findings from a previous Economic and Social Research Council-funded investigation into the media coverage of the release of General Certificate of Secondary Education and Advanced-level General Certificate of Education results, the paper builds on the findings of that study to explore wider implications. The earlier study had revealed the use of some standard 'media templates', which led to a fairly predictable range of news stories whatever the pattern of results might be in any given year. This paper explores ways in which Awarding Organisations and others might be more proactive in trying to improve the way in which assessments and examinations are portrayed in the media. It also considers the wider implications of the role of the media in influencing the public understanding of assessment issues.

Introduction

Each summer's release of General Certificate of Secondary Education (GCSE, usually taken by 16-year-olds) and Advanced-level General Certificate of Education (A-level, usually pre-university) examination results tends to be accompanied by UK media coverage, which is relatively extensive and which has a tendency to craft a major sensational story about some aspect of the rather arid statistics produced by the various awarding bodies (Warmington & Murphy, 2004). In 2012 the story that dominated the media coverage related to a reduction in the proportion of candidates achieving Grade C or better in some English GCSE examinations, accompanied by reports of grade boundaries being deliberately made harder either by the regulatory body for qualifications, examinations and assessments in England, Ofqual, or the Secretary of State (or indeed both working together). Within hours this story began to escalate in both volume and intensity, leading to coordinated action by teachers' associations to gather evidence, calls for legal action to be taken on the grounds of discrimination against certain sub-groups of students, and statements from Ofqual announcing that they would mount an immediate investigation into what had happened (Ofqual, 2012). Given that results in examinations of this type are almost bound to fluctuate up or down somewhat from year to year, it is interesting to reflect on how such stories can come to grab the attention of both the media and the general public and in many cases escalate to a level where they can dominate both national and local news coverage over a period of several days. Regardless of the year and the particular, often sensational, examination related stories that can emerge, I want to reflect upon why it is that such a large amount of journalistic time and space should so regularly be associated with the annual release of some tables of statistics that might on the face of it make only slightly more interesting reading than a telephone directory, or a digest of weather statistics.

There are, I think, several factors that contribute to this phenomenon which has in recent years become part of the national calendar. First, public examination results are for each student receiving them a very visible and critical representation of the outcomes of something like 11 to 13 years of schooling, and they are also very high stakes for their teachers, schools and colleges, as well as the Awarding Organisations, Ofqual, and even government ministers, because judgements are often made about their performance based upon the particular results issued in a given year. Above all the future progress of individual students into a next phase of education or in some cases employment can hang on a difference of just one grade in one subject. Getting a GCSE Grade D rather than a C in English will for many destroy their chances of moving on to post-16 educational courses and/or further training schemes or even employment. Getting an A-level Grade B, rather than an A, can lose others the chance to follow their chosen degree course or secure a place at a particular leading university.

Secondly, public examination results are arrived at by a set of quite complicated processes, which are not well understood by the general public, and there is therefore plenty of scope for public confidence in them to be rocked if there is any suggestion that something has 'gone wrong' with the marking and grade awarding processes. The processes of educational assessment involved in producing public examination grades involve all sorts of compromises, because it is not possible to come up with a single straightforward correct result for every student in every subject (Murphy et al., 1996; Murphy, 2004). Those involved in their production know only too well that they are only approximate measures, and are best viewed as having degrees of uncertainty attached to them. At the end of the day individual students will perform quite well or quite badly depending upon a wide range of factors, some of which relate to being lucky/unlucky with the examination questions that come up. As well as those factors examination marking and grading processes also rely heavily on human judgements, which can easily make a big difference to where any individual student falls in relation to particular grade boundaries, which themselves have to be placed according to all sorts of tricky judgements in relation to the difficulty of a particular examination.

The third factor, and this is, I suggest, rather different from the first two, relates to the general shortage of big media stories in the popular holiday month of August, when the public examination results are released. Those who have made the study of media reporting a specialist interest often refer to the holiday period around the month of August as 'the silly season' in terms of the type of stories that can be given prominence, due to the general lack of serious politically and socially important stories arising at this time of year when parliament is not sitting and large numbers of people are away taking their annual holidays. It is well documented through research conducted into the media coverage of public examination results in the UK, that the media rely upon getting prominent news stories out of the GCSE and A-level results days in mid-August, more or less regardless of the actual pattern of those results in any particular year.

One especially memorable year was 2002 when the release of the first A-level results following an initiative called Curriculum 2000 led to such media frenzy about alleged injustices that in time both the Secretary of State for Education, Estelle Morris, and the Chief Executive of the Qualifications and Curriculum Authority (QCA), Ken Boston, had to tender their resignations (McCaig, 2003; Warmington et al., 2005). Ten years later the media quickly picked up on concerns that some English GCSE results in particular had been 'marked down' in some way, causing a drop in the proportion of students gaining grade C or better. This fuelled speculation that this was both unjust and might have resulted either directly or indirectly from interference by Michael Gove, the Secretary of State for Education. Michael Gove was known to regard GCSE examinations as being 'too easy' and had talked repeatedly about both the dangers of what he regarded as 'grade inflation' (the pattern of improved results from one year to the next) and the need to reform what he describes as a 'discredited examination system' by forcing the Awarding Bodies and the regulator Ofqual to develop harder syllabuses, harder examinations, and results more like those produced under the old O-level system, which restricted the award of the higher grades to a much smaller proportion of students (DfE, 2012).

In this article I want to refer to each of these contributory causes of the sensationalisation of the reporting of GCSE and A-level results in more detail. I will do this both by looking back at the implications of a major study that I conducted on this topic some ten or so years ago (Warmington & Murphy, 2004) and by relating that discussion to the broader theme, being addressed through the other papers in this collection, which is the public understanding of assessment.

At the current time we do not have a very strong body of research evidence to help us fully understand the nature of the public understanding of educational assessment, but I want to highlight this media coverage research as one important piece of evidence that has significant implications for the wider discussions. The study to which I want to refer was conducted around ten years ago and was designed to investigate the way that the annual release of GCE and GCSE public examination results had been covered by the UK media. Although that research study was a decade ago it still stands out as being a unique pioneering piece of educational assessment research through the way that it looked at the popular portrayal of assessment issues, as part of the daily news reporting through print and broadcast media. Before getting into the specifics of that research I would first like to contextualise it within the broader setting of research that has been conducted into educational assessment in the UK, and the types of questions that need to be addressed in order to develop an informed discussion of perspectives in the public understanding of educational assessment.

Educational assessment results are, in marketing terms, a brand which depends very much on the confidence of the consumer. A-level examinations, for example, have regularly been described as the 'gold standard' upon which confidence in the performance of students from England, Wales and Northern Ireland, along with a large number of other countries, are judged. Multiple attempts to reform the A-level examination system have faltered on the grounds that there is much public trust in the A-level brand and if that were to be taken away the public might have difficulty in developing trust in whatever was put in its place. A recent example of this phenomenon was the eventual rejection of the proposals of the Tomlinson Committee (Working Group on 14–19 Reform, 2004), which recommended a new system of Diploma qualifications. The failure of the Tomlinson reform proposals followed a long line of similar rejections including the Higginson proposals for reform in the 1980s (DES, 1988) and several other failed attempts to reform A-level before that (Kingdon, 1991).

So we have A-level examinations as a strong brand, and in the early years of the GCE examination system we also had O-level examinations as the younger brother of A-levels, and also seen as a strong brand. The attempts to complement other reforms in the education system by widening access to public examinations led first to the introduction of CSE examinations and later to the merger of GCE and CSE examinations to form the new GCSE examinations, which came into existence some 25 years ago (Horton, 1987). Such has been the commitment to the A-level and O-level brands that even now there are many users of examination grades, who have difficulty in knowing what value to place on the results of 'modern examinations' such as GCSE.

The situation described above presents a picture of a public which knows what it likes, having grown used to a certain type of product, and which is potentially nervous of anything that might be introduced as an alternative mechanism for reporting on the achievements of students. This situation does not depend upon technical debates about question papers, marking schemes and the setting of grade boundaries; it depends much more on consumer confidence in a brand that has been around for a while and has been seen to work. All of this fits with the nature of the examination industry, which does not especially seek to share the intricacies of setting, marking and grading public examinations with the general public. 'Trust us—we are the experts in this business and we know what we are doing' would be a possible way of portraying the stance of the big Awarding Organisations, which still bear the weight of responsibility for the conduct of the high stakes public examinations that have dominated the English education system for over 60 years. The annual media coverage of the results release days in August takes on added significance in the context that this may be the most extensive discussion to which the general public is exposed. If public examinations are largely out of the public gaze for 364 days of the year, then it is not difficult to argue that what is said and written, on and around the annual release date, may have a very significant influence in the public's general knowledge and understanding of these very influential qualifications.

The media coverage of examinations—the Economic and Social Research Council (ESRC) study

In the only major research study looking at the media coverage of UK examination results (Warmington & Murphy, 2004, 2007) we undertook a very detailed systematic study of both print and media coverage of the release of GCSE and A-level results in two successive years. We were interested to take a careful look at exactly how examination results were portrayed around the dates when the bulk of the UK school examination results are released each August. We were aware that there were likely to be differences between print and broadcast media and between local and national reporting, and we prepared for this study by immersing ourselves in the mainly sociological literature, which has analysed the role of the media in communicating topical social issues to the general public. The previous publications arising from that project have outlined both the detailed methods that we employed and the painstaking analysis that we performed on several hundred items of media coverage. The conclusions that we were able to draw from all of that were both alarming and challenging for anyone with aspirations to try to improve the public understanding of assessment issues.

The picture that emerged was of very extensive coverage of examination results, at a time of year when news stories tend to be in short supply. However, the fact that it was extensive did not necessarily lead to it being highly detailed and informative. Much of it was at a relatively simple level and was constructed around some well used and familiar 'media templates'. Many accounts included the more or less obligatory photographs of ecstatic successful students hugging each other and engaging in wild celebrations. From there the story frequently moved quickly towards an often forensic exploration of the value of the results obtained, and many references to doubts about whether the freshly released results were on a par with those issued in previous years. 'Grade inflation' and 'dumbing down' have become popular organising concepts for reporting these examinations results, and in recent years they have been joined by 'the race to the bottom' as a commentary on the relative standing of examination results issued by different Awarding

Organisations, in different subjects and in different years. Our research design included interviews with education correspondents and others with a deep knowledge of the way that media operate. Such people offered an enlightening view of the way in which examination results are classified as news before they are ever released. News editors, searching for news stories in the middle of the news-starved summer vacation, would allocate column inches and news bulletin minutes, ahead of knowing whether there was anything particularly out of the ordinary in the overall patterns emerging from the latest national results data. In summary one can be more or less certain that there is likely be a big media story arising from the release of results, which occurs on two successive Thursdays in mid-August with the A-level results coming out first. The much more difficult question to predict is what that story will be, and whether any of the key stakeholders will attempt, and be successful in their attempts, to steer the media coverage in one particular direction or another.

The overall conclusions of our ESRC-funded research project were that the media reporting of public examination results was dominated by a restricted set of structural, narrative and presentation templates, which at the time were dominated by a 'standards are falling' mantra that could be developed in relation to less good results as well as improved results. The way this appeared to work was that, if the results in any subject exam got worse, then it was self-evident that the standard of candidates' work had diminished. On the other hand if the results appeared to have improved then by a subtle twist of logic the media would tweak the story so that it would suggest that the exams must be getting easier, and therefore reflected falling standards in students' achievements. This ability to turn either an improvement or a decline into the same 'standards are falling' template is fully encapsulated in a classic quotation from the *Financial Times* around the time of our original study:

> Terrible news from north and south of the border: our education system is falling apart. In Scotland, this is demonstrated by a slump in the pass rate ... in England and Wales, it is an increase in the A-Level pass rate which leads to the same conclusion. (*Financial Times*, 15 August 2003)

Clearly the 'falling standards' template is not the only one employed, and in the years since our earlier work the media has delighted in highlighting 'examination paper errors', 'examination board mishaps', and even 'dodgy practices designed to manipulate grade outcomes'. As with the reporting of other issues relating to education, the general stance is normally a negative one and as time has gone by the volume of coverage of education issues in the media has been greatly increased (Wallace, 1993; Jeffs, 1999). The picture that has emerged from our own and other peoples' analyses of this type of media reporting is one of predictability, negativity and of limited perspectives.

> A-Level stories, and their subtext, are predictable. By the time you read this, the highest ever proportion of good A-Level passes will have been recorded; ignorant commentators will have trumpeted that A-Levels and GCSEs have been 'dumbed down';

ministers will have piously responded that we should 'celebrate the achievements' of our children. (*New Statesman*, 18 August 2003)

In recent years with a new government and a Secretary of State who is openly critical of public examinations, teachers, state schools and educational standards in general, the right-wing newspapers have found support rather than opposition from government ministers in their attacks on the Awarding Organisations, examination syllabuses, assessment schemes and results. Michael Gove has been reported as being attracted by the possibility of returning to a two-tier examination system with something resembling O-Level and CSE examinations. He is also known to be deeply suspicious of examination results which in any way suggest that students are achieving better outcomes, and is desperate to halt 'grade inflation' and what has been described as the 'race to the bottom', with awarding bodies allegedly competing with each other to offer 'easier' examinations in order to attract a bigger market share. The arrival on the scene of Ofqual, which is the newly created examinations regulator, and Pearson, the commercial publishing company which took over Edexcel, which is one of the three big unitary Awarding Organisations in England, has all added spice to journalistic accounts which tend still to be inclined to look for controversy, corruption and underhand practices when it comes to reporting stories related to examinations. The landscape of assessment in England is continually changing and to understand what is going on, in an educated way, the public, and indeed education professionals, need access to informed accounts of significant changes, which critically appraise the changing dynamics as well as describing them in a factual way.

Another conclusion from our earlier studies on the reporting of examination results was that the media are themselves a complex conglomeration of different parts and practices. In the UK we have a very extensive array of national newspapers, many of which have clear political affiliations, and that affects the angle they take on issues related to examinations. Alongside the national papers we have an extensive array of more local newspapers and they as a whole are much more likely to report good news examination stories, generally relating to the examination successes of individual local students or local schools. Then alongside the print media we have the broadcast media, within which there is further diversity especially in relation to those publicly funded broadcasters, who have statutory obligation to maintain balance in the way that they report news items with constraints in relation to avoiding explicit editorialisation (BBC, 2003; ITC, 2003). Cottle (1995), Williams (1997) and others have also explored the role of 'contest' in shaping broadcast reporting of potentially controversial items. In the case of examination results and the falling standards template, this frequently is played out in television studios, where two pundits with opposing views on the meaning of a new set of examination results trade verbal blows over whether such a thing can be taken as in any way showing legitimate improvements in students' educational achievements. Getting two people with extreme oppositional views to debate with each other is one way of trying to present a balanced picture, but it is not the only way and it leads potentially to the danger of over-representing extreme viewpoints rather than more commonly held more balanced viewpoints. It also can exacerbate the problem of leaving the viewing/listening audience confused about something that they might have thought they understood better before they experienced that particular radio or television coverage. Also, because broadcast exchanges of this kind are generally rather brief, they can rely heavily on rather simplistic condensations of complex issues, and what Williams (1997) and others have termed 'polarised discourse'. If we apply this idea to a television studio discussion of recently released examination results the impact may be that the viewing public get to witness a lively exchange between two pundits with opposite views about whether for example some improvement in examination grade outcomes can be taken to signal a genuine educational improvement. At the end of the item they may be left with little in terms of new insights into what is quite a complex matter. Wallace (1993) talks about this, in terms of broadcast media turning debates about important social issues into some kind of 'spectacle', with the danger that the outcome is that viewers/listeners are provided with good entertainment, rather than becoming better informed about a relatively complex matter. In a similar vein Curran (2000) critiques the supposed information public service role of the media, and talks about entertainment, spectacle and myth-making as key media products.

There is clearly a danger in discussions like these to portray the media as the culprits and the rest of us as the victims. That of course is unfair and neglects the responsibility of those involved in assessment and examining to play a more effective role in influencing the media to ensure that the public is presented with a better informed view of vitally important issues that influence the way in which assessment results are both produced, reported and understood.

The public understanding of assessment issues

I now want to go on to some more general reflections about the public understanding of assessment issues and relate that to the specific work that I have been discussing about the media coverage of assessment results. Other papers in this collection have noted how restricted the public understanding of assessment issues is, and the current reflection on media coverage issues provides an interesting insight into why this may be so, as well as contributing to our understanding of some of the implications of our situation, where the public understanding of assessment issues is so ill-informed.

The shallowness of media reporting around assessment results could not occur in a context where the public were better informed about matters, such as the grading of GCSE and GCE examinations. In the height of the media frenzy that followed the 2002 release of A-Level grades the *Daily Mail* newspaper ran a front page headline of 'YOU CHEATS' supported by an inside page headline 'SCANDAL OF GRADE ROBBERS'. In 2012 the furore about GCSE English grading standards hinged on issues such as whether there had been any political interference in the instructions given to examiners before they started marking the particular examination papers. Those familiar with how GCE and GCSE examinations are marked and graded are more than aware that grading decisions are only made after the marking process has finished and the placing of grade boundaries is always subject to a variety of checks and balances. The reality is that each grade boundary in each subject effectively has to be signed off by the designated Responsible Officer within each Awarding Body, and now there is an examinations regulator, Ofqual, as well. All of this means that the 'shock horror' associated with stories about grading decisions being influenced by people other than the examiners who mark the papers is in effect for the most part a sensationalisation of what are normal Awarding Organisation processes applied as a routine aspect of awarding every public examination grade. There are I think two main conclusions that can be made here. First, the rather stereotypical and often simplistic template driven reporting on examination results seems to feed off the fact that the general public has no real idea how exam grades are arrived at. Thus any suggestion that grades depend on more than a mark assigned by each examiner, who marks each script, can be the basis for fuelling suspicion about the grade awarding processes. Secondly, the way that such reporting occurs probably does more to undermine the public understanding of assessment issues than it does to promote it. If the media present debates about, say, grading standards in a polarised oppositional way relying on simplistic icon words, then such reporting does little to contribute to a better informed public understanding of assessment issues.

Another important issue to raise in relation to improving the public understanding of assessment issues is to consider whether the quality of reporting about examination results could be influenced further by those who have aspirations for the public to be better informed about this important feature of the education system in England, Wales and Northern Ireland. Here it is important to heed the warnings of Mike Baker, who was himself a very experienced former BBC education correspondent. Baker (2000) spoke eloquently about the problem created by an apparent almost total disengagement of educational professionals from the harsh realities of how the media operate.

> ... education gets exactly the sort of media it deserves because educators make so little effort to influence the message and have therefore abandoned the public ... debate to the politicians and polemicists. (Baker, 2000)

In our own work on the media coverage of assessment results we interacted a great deal with staff from awarding bodies and government agencies, who on the face of it had much to gain from trying to influence the way in which examinations issues were reported in the media, and we ended up concluding from these interactions that on the whole such people were:

(1) Poorly informed about how the media operate.
(2) Largely motivated by a fear of what the media might write.
(3) Pessimistic about the chances of gaining constructive media coverage.

(4)   Seriously underachieving in terms of influencing the impact of the media on the public understanding of assessment issues.

This is not to imply that working towards getting better media coverage in relation to assessment issues is an easy process. We are more than aware of how the best intentions to influence media coverage can go seriously wrong, especially if this is seen by the media as an indication that a more serious story is being suppressed or deliberately kept from the public consciousness. It is certainly difficult to replace bad news reporting with good news reporting for reasons that Baker himself has explained.

> ... media tends to concentrate on those areas where things are not working as well as they might ... News is not a mirror reflecting everything as it is. News is about the exceptional, not the ordinary. It is a spotlight on areas which are new, interesting, troublesome, problematic, exciting. (Baker, 2000)

As well as tending towards the negative the media tends to like simplified debates rather than complex debates. The challenge is therefore for educators involved in assessment work to make the key issues more accessible to the general public, and as one part of that work to try to encourage the media towards better informed reporting about assessment issues. This in my view will involve actions such as:

(a)   Developing a deeper understanding of how the media operate.
(b)   Investing more resources in getting better media coverage, especially by employing professional staff with considerable prior experience in that type of work.
(c)   Being proactive rather than reactive, including looking for much more media coverage away from the highly charged release dates for annual results.
(d)   Taking on the challenge of making complex matters reasonably accessible to an audience, which may have very little understanding of educational assessment issues, practices and techniques.
(e)   Being prepared for a bumpy ride, because things rarely come out in the media in the way that those seeking coverage intend, and a track record of success will usually have had a few calamities along the way.

There is a lot of good work going on to develop useful, effective and educative assessment systems that only currently receives a tiny fraction of the media coverage, which is allocated to the more sensational stories arising from the annual release of examination results. If a greater public understanding of assessment issues is to be achieved then a better balanced diet of assessment coverage is needed in the media, and those working to promote such a shift need to find ways to take a new agenda to news journalists and try to get them to engage with some of the more positive trends in initiatives such as 'Assessment For Learning' and the work that the Awarding Organisations and Assessment Agencies are doing to promote modern approaches to educational assessment which are fairer, more valid and more likely to promote effective learning. In the years since our original study in this area it is certainly the case that the Awarding Organisations have become more skilled in the area of communications with the public. The fact that some progress has been made should not, however, lead to complacency, as there is still a long way to go, if the public is to be helped to understand educational assessment issues better. There are at the moment promising signs that the new social media opportunities are beginning to allow different types of dialogue to occur and that these more than others can be driven by the genuine interests of students, parents and teachers, rather than being manipulated by media barons and media-wise politicians. There is no doubt that any debate about the public understanding of assessment issues needs to take account of the important role played by the media, and as in so many areas of education the media can play a constructive role, if educational professionals know how to best go about helping them to do that.

References

Baker, M. (2000). *Does education get the media it deserves?* Inaugural Lecture, Institute of Education, University of London.

British Broadcasting Corporation (2003). Impartiality and accuracy, in: *BBC Producers' Guidelines*. Available online at: http://www.bbc.co.uk/guidelines/editorialguidelines/edguide/impariality/ (accessed January 2007).

Cottle, S. (1995). The production of news formats: determinants of mediated public contestation. *Media, Culture and Society*, 17, 275–291.

Curran, J. (2000). Rethinking media and democracy, in: J. Curran & M. Gurevitch (Eds) *Mass media and society*. London, Arnold, 120–154.

Department for Education (2012). *Reforming Key Stage 4 qualifications*. Circular, September 17.

Department of Education and Science/Welsh Office (1988). *Advancing A Levels: report of a committee appointed by the Secretary of State for Education and Science and the Secretary of State for Wales* (The Higginson Report). London, HMSO.

Horton, T. (1987). GCSE: *examining the new system*. London, Harper & Row.

Independent Television Commission (ITC) (2003). Impartiality, in: *ITC programme code*. Available online at: http://www.ofcom.org.uk/static/archive/itc/itc_publications/codes_guidance/programme_code/section_3.asp.html (accessed January 2007).

Jeffs, T. (1999). Are you paying attention? Education and the media, in: B. Franklin (Ed.) *Social policy, the media and misrepresentation*. London, Routledge.

Kingdon, M (1991). *The reform of Advanced Level*. London, Hodder & Stoughton.

McCaig, C. (2003). School exams: leavers in panic. *Parliamentary Affairs*, 56(3), 471–489. Available online at: http://dx.doi.org/10.1093/parlij/gsg101

Murphy, R. (2004). *Grades of uncertainty*. London, Association of Teachers and Lecturers.

Murphy, R., Wilmut, J. & Wood, R. (1996). Monitoring A-level Standards: tests, grades and other approximations. *The Curriculum Journal*, 7(3), 279–291.

Ofqual (2012). *GCSE English awards 2012: a regulatory report*. Coventry, Ofqual.

Wallace, M. (1993). Discourse of derision: the role of mass media within the education policy process. *Journal of Education Policy*, 8(4), 321–337.

Warmington, P. & Murphy, R. (2004). Could do better? Media depictions of UK educational assessment results. *Journal of Education Policy*, 19(3), 285–299. Available online at: http://dx.doi.org/10.1080/0268093042000207629

Warmington, P. & Murphy, R. (2007). 'Read all about it!' UK news media coverage of A-Level Results. *Policy Futures in Education*, 5(1), 70–83.

Warmington, P., Murphy, R. & McCaig, C. (2005). Real and imagined crises: the construction of political and media panics over education. *British Educational Research Association Research Intelligence*, 90, 12–14.

Williams, J. (1997). *Negotiating access to higher education: the discourse of selectivity and equity*. Buckingham, Open University Press/Society for Research into Higher Education.

Working Group on 14–19 Reform (2004). *14–19 curriculum and qualification reform* (Tomlinson Report). London, Department for Education and Skills.

Index

INDEX